IDA B. WELLS-BARNETT: WOMAN OF COURAGE

Yours truly

Ida B. Wells.

IDA B. WELLS-BARNETT
Woman of Courage

BY ELIZABETH VAN STEENWYK

Franklin Watts
New York   London   Toronto   Sydney
An Impact Biography

Photographs copyright ©: University of Chicago Library, Special Collections: pp. frontis (portrait), 1, 9, 13, 14; Paul Lee/Best Efforts, Inc.: pp. frontis (signature), 2, 4, 5, 6, 7, 10, 11, 12; New York Public Library, Schomburg Center for Research in Black Culture: pp. 3, 16; Archive Photos, NYC: p. 8.

Library of Congress Cataloging-in-Publication Data

Van Steenwyk, Elizabeth.
Ida B. Wells-Barnett: woman of courage/by Elizabeth Van Steenwyk.
p. cm.—(An Impact biography)
Includes bibliographical references and index.
Summary: A biography of the black woman who campaigned for civil rights and founded the National Association for the Advancement of Colored People.
ISBN 0-531-13014-2
1. Wells-Barnett, Ida B., 1862-1931—Juvenile literature.   2. Afro-Americans—Biography—Juvenile literature.   3.   Afro-American women—Biography—Juvenile literature.   4.   Civil rights workers—United States—Biography—Juvenile literature.   [1. Wells-Barnett, Ida B., 1862-1931.
2. Civil rights workers.   3.   Afro-Americans—Biography.]
I. Title.
E185.97.W55V36   1992
323'.092—dc20   91-35019 CIP AC
[B]

CONTENTS

DEDICATED TO MY FRIEND
BEAUFORD POWELL

Special thanks to the following: Barbara Simon, for her computer expertise, her advice, friendship, and never ending patience; to librarians Beverly Nairne and Mary Richardson for their assistance; and to Dr. Troy Duster and Mr. Benjamin Duster in providing warm family ties to the great lady.

IDA B. WELLS-BARNETT: WOMAN OF COURAGE

"Let your songs be songs of faith and hope."

Ida B. Wells-Barnett
January 1922

1
THE EARLY YEARS

The summer of 1862 in Washington, D.C., grew increasingly hot and humid as June gave way to July. Already it was the second summer of the Civil War—and government officials on both sides thought it should have ended after the first.

At the battle of Bull Run, the Union Army was routed from the Virginia countryside by the Confederates. It was no longer a Picture Book War.[1] Politicians and their wives no longer drove their carriages out to the country, then spread picnics on blankets to watch soldiers ride on well-groomed horses and play at battle. Soldiers really bled and died. Wives became widows. Children became orphans.

Now, in this summer of 1862, the man in the White House—gaunt, sober Abraham Lincoln—paced his office as he suffered for each soldier he sent to war. At first, his only motive had been to save the Union, but soon he realized that he must officially abolish slavery as well. He said that he was "now convinced that this was a great movement of God to end slavery."[2]

With the Republican Congress, Lincoln had begun to chip away at the institution of slavery, first by abolishing it in the capital, then by forbidding Union officers to return slaves to their owners, and, finally, by outlawing slavery in all federal territories.

But it wasn't enough. Lincoln worried that an official proclamation was "too big a lick"[3] and would push the border states of Missouri, Kentucky, and Maryland over to the side of the Confederacy. He realized that something drastic needed to be done if the Union was going to win the war. On July 4, Senator Charles Sumner of Massachusetts called at the White House to urge Lincoln that a decree emancipating all blacks from slavery was needed. In his own mind the president already had begun to compose it.

Twelve days later, on July 16, 1862, in Holly Springs, Mississippi, a baby girl was born to Jim and Elizabeth Wells, who were slaves and married as such. They named their first child Ida Bell and hoped her life would be an improvement over their own, although they had not suffered as many indignities as other slaves they knew.

Jim Wells, Ida's father, was half African-American, half white. His father was his master, who owned a plantation not far away in Tippah County. Jim's mother was a slave woman on the estate. Since Jim grew up on his father's plantation, he was never whipped or sold. When he reached eighteen, his father apprenticed him to Mr. Bolling, a carpenter, to learn that trade. Jim Wells was expected to return to work on his father's estate once his apprenticeship ended.

Ida Bell's mother was born in Virginia as Elizabeth Warrenton. One of ten children, she was only seven when slave traders took her to Mississippi where she was sold several times before being purchased by Bolling. Many years later Elizabeth told her own children that her father was half Indian, but she was never able to trace her family roots.

12

Elizabeth grew up to be the cook for Bolling, and it was in his house that she met and married Jim. When the war ended, Jim and Elizabeth married again, as freed citizens. Bolling asked his assistant to stay with him and to work in the construction business, which Jim Wells did.

The events prior to Ida Bell's birth and during her formative years would have a profound effect not only on her life, but on all members of her race for generations to come.

The president's edict, begun in July 1862, proceeded through many drafts before the final one, known as the Emancipation Proclamation, was signed into law on January 1, 1863. That day became known as the Day of Jubilee to all African-Americans. Later the proclamation became the Thirteenth Amendment to the Constitution of the United States.

Even as the divided nation struggled during four years of civil war, President Lincoln was already thinking ahead to the future. He struggled with the problem of putting the nation back together again once the fighting ended. A general policy of reconstruction needed to be developed, and Lincoln felt the job belonged to the president.

On December 8, 1863, Lincoln issued his Proclamation of Amnesty and Reconstruction. In it he offered a pardon to any former Confederate who would take an oath of loyalty to support the Constitution of the United States. There were certain exceptions, most of them involving military officers who had resigned commissions in the United States and aided in the Confederate rebellion.

Lincoln wanted to implement the program on a gradual basis. As more and more of the Confederacy came under Union control through military victories, he gave Union officers authority to administer the oath and to pardon Confederate soldiers, hoping the machinery of reconstruction would be operating efficiently at the end of the war.

The members of the Congress saw Reconstruction differently, however, feeling the president was too forgiving and had overstepped his executive duties. They felt he should leave political reorganization to Congress and suppress an armed rebellion from the South with arms, not conciliatory action.

The war ended with General Robert E. Lee signing a surrender treaty dictated by the Union's General Ulysses S. Grant at Appomattox Court House, Virginia, on April 9, 1865. Six days later, Abraham Lincoln lay dead of an assassin's bullet. It was up to the new president, Andrew Johnson, to bring about a period of amnesty and reconstruction. Although his position differed little from Lincoln's, he lacked the late president's statesmanship.

The North greatly mourned the loss of its wartime leader, but rejoiced in the overwhelming victory it had achieved. Prosperous conditions greeted the soldiers of the North when they returned home. The warm reception buoyed their spirits and encouraged them to make ambitious plans for the future.

As the weary, hungry soldiers of the Confederacy returned to their homes, however, the conditions that greeted them were totally different. Destruction was everywhere. During the last days of the war, the Confederates retreated before the onrushing Union army, burning homes, buildings, and supplies that might be useful to the enemy. What they didn't destroy, the army in blue did. As Carl Schurz, a Republican leader traveling in the South later remarked, the countryside "looked for many miles like a broad black streak of ruin and desolation...."[4]

For the Confederates then, the past was a painful memory, the present unendurable, and the future grim. The economy of those eleven states[5] waiting for readmission to the Union had been smashed, and there was little with which to rebuild. But if the white Southerners were defeated militarily and materially, their spirit survived. They remained fiercely loyal to their former way of life in which white men ruled and ruled totally. Although not all Southerners were plantation owners, all those who could afford it had owned slaves to help farm a piece of land. Land was what Southerners loved and what they knew would endure. Although much of it had been scorched, it had not been destroyed.

The white Southerners went to work, and by autumn of 1865, when Ida was three years old, Reconstruction in the South was in the hands of ex-Confederates as well as other Southerners who had not been secessionists. President Johnson's plans for restructuring allowed the Southern states to hold conventions and form new state governments while giving blacks little voice in the process of Reconstruction.

Conditions for African-Americans improved temporarily once the Freedman's Bureau was established. Created by Congress just before the end of the war, the Bureau was designed to help refugees and freed men and women to receive supplies and medical help, to establish new and equal schools, and to bridge the gap between employees and employers.

Increasingly, white Southerners grew more hostile toward the Bureau. Ex-Confederates called it "an engine of mischief,"[6] feeling that it stood in the way of the states' rights and self-government. The former Confederate states did not want to seem overly compliant on the slavery question. Former owners agreed to abolish slavery by legislation but expected to be monetarily compensated for their losses. Nor were they receptive to the idea that black men should be given their *franchise*, or right to vote.

After the Southern states took economic steps to attract new business, they created a public education

15

system. But this system was designed for white citizens only. Laws passed by the new state governments, called black codes, were increasingly unfair. Although African-Americans could own property, they could not be considered witnesses in any legal proceeding unless one or both parties were black. They could not marry whites. Contracts between black workers and white employers became increasingly one-sided. Many communities allowed African-Americans on the streets only during certain hours, and blacks could not be ordained ministers of the gospel without a license.

More and more, blacks were restricted, and they were fined heavily if they were found breaking the rules. Gradually, white groups such as the Regulators, Jayhawkers, and Black Horse Cavalry were formed to harass and terrorize blacks. African-American schools were damaged and burned down. The Confederacy may have been beaten, but its philosophy of white supremacy wouldn't die.

Finally, in Washington, D.C., a Joint Committee of Fifteen was formed. Made up of nine representatives and six senators, the committee's directive was to investigate conditions in the ex-Confederate states. As members gathered information about the treatment of blacks in the South, testimony convinced them that safeguards were needed before the former Confederate states could once again be fully represented in the United Sates legislature. In April 1866, the Joint Committee devised a set of resolutions that were introduced as the Fourteenth Amendment, giving blacks the right to citizenship, although it still did not guarantee them the right to vote.

Sometime in 1867 African-Americans in Mississippi were given voting rights. However, it was not until 1870, when the Fifteenth Amendment to the Constitution of the United States was ratified, that all male citizens in all states were given the right to vote.

By the same year, 1870, all eleven Confederate states

had been re-admitted to the Union. The Republicans, who had little voice in the South before the war, now controlled every new state government.

There were three groups of Republicans, the largest group being black. Thousands now voted, but no state elected a black governor, and only seventeen African-Americans were elected to Congress.

Many Northerners came south to find new economic opportunities and soon also became involved in Republican government. They were known as *carpetbaggers* because it was thought they could fit all their possessions into a suitcase, or carpetbag, when they moved south.

The third group was made up of poor white Southerners who were called scalawags. They resented the formerly rich plantation owners and, in state government, sided with blacks and carpetbaggers.

One of the programs which the states now took over from the Freedman's Bureau was the school system. Many new schools were built, and young and old blacks enthusiastically enrolled, although most whites refused to attend. Later, the states would segregate the schools, even though it was against the law.

Many Southern whites refused to support this Reconstruction government, considering it illegal because the Fourteenth Amendment prevented many Southerners from holding office. Even more, the Southerners had difficulty accepting blacks in their new roles. Gradually, whites stayed away from elections. Many turned to violence. United States troops intervened, but they had little success against groups such as the Ku Klux Klan.

A group of young white men had organized the Ku Klux Klan in Pulaski, Tennessee, shortly after the end of the Civil War. Within months, this secret lodge began to terrorize blacks, swooping down in the dark of night to raid homes and businesses, while wearing the guise of white costumes and masks. Other chapters, or dens, were formed, and officers carried strange titles such as dragon, fury, titan, and nighthawk. Soon it was apparent that the Klan wanted to do more than just frighten blacks. It wanted to reestablish full white supremacy. Not only did they terrorize blacks; they ostracized and intimidated them, bought or stole their votes, and glorified the white race. The Klan continues its prejudicial practices to this day.

When Jim Wells prepared to vote for the first time, Bolling told him to vote the Democratic ticket. Wells refused and while he was at the polling place, Bolling locked him out of the shop. Jim Wells went to town and bought himself some carpenter's tools, then rented a house across the street from Bolling, moved his family into it, and set up his own business. A case could be made that the spirit of strong-willed independence which Ida Bell would display throughout her life was inherited directly from her father.

The same year that her father exercised his franchise for the first time, Ida Bell entered school, although she said she had no clear recollection of the exact time or place.[7] According to her daughter Alfreda Barnett Duster, Ida spent all her school years at Rust College in Holly Springs, Mississippi, and was considered a very bright student.

Rust College, originally called Shaw University, was founded in 1866 by a Northern minister, Reverend A. C. McDonald. In those days, Rust offered an education at all levels and grades, including basic elementary studies. Since Ida's parents insisted that their children should be educated, they sent Ida to Rust so she would benefit from the teachings of the missionaries who came south to Holly Springs after dedicating themselves to helping freed men and women. These teachers believed in teaching puritanical values of hard work and devotion to

18

duty with a curriculum that included European history and culture.

Ida's first memories were of reading the newspaper to her father and his friends, then listening to their discussions. Since they were interested in politics, she encountered many terms not found in her reading books at school, among them, the name *Ku Klux Klan*. As her father took on an increasing role in political rallies and meetings, Ida assumed, as she later stated in her autobiography, that blacks were now considered equal with whites. Many of her father's friends were active in government, among them James Hill, who became Mississippi's secretary of state when Ida was twelve.

By the early 1870s, however, the ex-Confederates of Mississippi (as well as in the rest of the South) began to drive all Republicans from power. During that time of tension, Ida knew that her mother sat up many nights, waiting for her father to return home from political meetings. Hundreds of blacks were killed in the South by the Ku Klux Klan in those years. Although Holly Springs was spared some of the violence, the threat was always real and ever near.

Despite repeated attempts by President Ulysses S. Grant to stop the violence against blacks, it continued as Southern Democrats slowly regained control of government. In addition, many Northerners were losing interest, allowing United States troops to begin withdrawing from the South.

The presidential election of 1876 represented the end of Reconstruction. When a compromise between Republicans and Democrats led to the withdrawal of the remaining U.S. troops in the South, Republican candidate Rutherford B. Hayes was elected president of the United States. Many African-Americans felt that the party of Abraham Lincoln had deserted them as Southern Democrats created what soon became known as the "Solid South." Forty years would pass before a Republican candidate for president would again receive a majority of votes in any Southern state.

During these years of Reconstruction, Ida Wells was growing up into a bright, serious young woman. She worked hard at school and at home as well, taking on many household chores as the family grew. Each Saturday night she helped bathe the younger children, shined their shoes, and laid out their best clothes. On Sunday mornings, the Wellses brought their seven children to Sunday School and even won a prize for regular attendance. Games were forbidden the rest of the day, and Ida could only read the Bible to the family.

Despite increasing political tensions, life seemed secure and comfortable for the Wells family. Jim built his family a house and worked regularly in Holly Springs. Not only was he well thought of as a skilled carpenter; he was highly regarded as a civic-minded citizen and served on the first board of trustees of Rust College, even though he was barely literate.

For Elizabeth Wells, who no longer worked in white people's kitchens, there was now time to raise her seven children and pursue another dream—learning to read. Elizabeth attended school with Ida until she learned to read the Bible without assistance.

It was a happy and reasonably secure beginning for Ida, but that suddenly ended the summer she turned sixteen.

2
A NEW AND
DIFFERENT WORLD

In the summer of 1878, when Ida turned sixteen, she went to visit her grandmother Peggy and her husband on the farm they purchased after emancipation.

Ida knew Grandmother Peggy well. Peggy came to Holly Springs each year to sell her cotton and corn and then visited her son, Jim, and his family. In turn the children visited their grandmother and other relatives who lived nearby.

The farm was deep in the country, near the old Wells plantation where Jim had been born and raised. There were no newspapers, and mail delivery was not dependable, so Ida and her relatives there were unaware that a yellow fever epidemic had broken out. It quickly spread through the Mississippi Valley from New Orleans, Louisiana, north as far as Memphis, Tennessee, fifty miles from Holly Springs.

No one knew yet what caused yellow fever, or yellow jack, as it was sometimes called. It seemed to strike without warning. The patient came down with a high fever, headache, and backache, often becoming more seriously ill with internal bleeding. In severe cases, death resulted. Because it was highly contagious and no one knew it was caused by a virus transmitted by certain mosquitoes, towns usually quarantined themselves against visitors when an outbreak occurred nearby.

Holly Springs had escaped previous yellow fever epidemics, since the illness usually confined itself to swampy lowlands where mosquitoes bred. In 1878, however, the mayor of Holly Springs decided to help refugees from Memphis who were trying to evade the epidemic. He welcomed them to Holly Springs.

The disease soon spread in Ida's hometown, and two thousand of its citizens quickly evacuated the town. Of the fifteen hundred that remained, all but one hundred contracted the disease. Three hundred citizens died before the epidemic finally subsided.

Relief organizations sent disaster and medical supplies plus doctors and nurses when news of the problem reached them. Many of the doctors had already survived yellow fever epidemics and were immune. They needed assistance, however, and some townspeople volunteered, among them Jim and Elizabeth Wells.

Out on Grandmother Peggy's farm, Ida wasn't concerned about her family in Holly Springs. She hadn't heard from them in a while, but she blamed the slow mail delivery for that. When she finally heard about the epidemic, she still didn't worry because she was sure that her father had taken the family out to the country to stay with Aunt Belle, her mother's sister, until the emergency ended.

One day in early fall, Ida heard someone call her name from the front gate of her grandmother's house. Looking outside, she recognized the three men on horseback as friends of her parents. Thinking they had come to pay a social call on her and her grandmother, she invited them in and eagerly asked for news of her family at home.

One of the men handed her a letter written by another friend of her parents. Ida read:

"Jim and Lizzie Wells have both died of the fever within twenty-four hours of each other. The children are all at home and the Howard Association has put a woman there to take care of them. Send word to Ida."[1]

Grandmother Peggy begged Ida to stay, at least not to return to Holly Springs until all danger of contracting the fever had passed. A great debate raged inside Ida. Maybe she should remain on the farm so she wouldn't become ill and could care for the children once the epidemic ended. But they needed her now, this minute, as well as next month and next year. The sixteen-year-old worried and waited.

Three days later, a second letter arrived. This one was written by a Doctor Gray, who urged her to return at once, for the sake of the children. Ida needed no more persuading; she caught the next train home. The caboose in which she rode was draped in black in memory of two conductors who had also succumbed to the fever.

A new and different world awaited Ida as she stepped from the train in Holly Springs. The vibrant, bustling little town she'd left a short time ago now lived in shadows and silence. Stores were closed, many gone out of business never to reopen, and the streets were empty except for the hearses which made daily trips to the cemetery.

Ida walked into her own home to find five frightened children waiting for her. Baby Stanley also had died in the epidemic. But Eugenia, a paralytic next in age to Ida; the boys, James and George, who were eleven and nine; Annie, aged five; and Lily, two years old, looked to Ida with sad, dark eyes, wondering what would happen to them.

First, though, Eugenia wanted to tell Ida what had happened. She said their father had worked hard at the courthouse, which had been turned into a temporary hospital. Gray reported that Jim Wells had prayed with the dying, soothed the feverish, and built coffins for the patients who didn't survive. When Elizabeth Wells became ill, he nursed her as well, and then the children, one by one, as they caught the fever. Finally, Jim came down with yellow jack and died the day before Elizabeth did.

A short time later, Dr. Gray came to the house and told Ida what a wonderful man her father had been. Then he gave her three hundred dollars which had belonged to her father and which Dr. Gray had been holding in safekeeping. Later, a nurse told Ida how Dr. Gray had watched out for the children until Ida arrived. "Dr. Gray sure is one good white man,"[2] the nurse said. Ida couldn't have agreed more.

One Sunday afternoon in November, after the epidemic had subsided, a group of Jim and Elizabeth's friends gathered in the Wells home. Jim Wells had been a Mason, and now his fellow lodge members wanted to help Ida decide what to do next. During the discussion among the adults, it was decided that one family would see the boys through apprenticeships, two other families would take Annie and Lily, and Ida was old enough to take care of herself. But no one wanted crippled Eugenia. She would have to go to the poorhouse.

It must have been difficult for Ida to listen to that discussion, but she did, without once interrupting. Then she spoke up. No one was going anywhere, she told them. The family would not be divided but would stay together, and she would be in charge. They owned the house they lived in, and her father had left some money on which they would manage while Ida found work.

Arguments erupted, but Ida refused to listen. Finally it must have occurred to everyone present that Ida meant what she said, and the lodge members let her have her way. Two of them were appointed guardians and advised Ida to seek employment as a country schoolteacher.

Ida wound her hair into a bun and let down her skirts to appear older, then took the teacher's exam and passed it. Soon, she received an appointment to a country school six miles out of town. For that job, she would be paid twenty-five dollars a month. At the age of sixteen, Ida was the employed head and sole breadwinner of a household of six.

Although Ida's closest friends had been the students and teachers at Rust College, she seemed to leave them behind easily, stepping into her new role without hesitation. Not until years later did she confide to someone what a difficult day it was when she knew her carefree days at Rust were ended. Now, on Sunday afternoons, instead of preparing for a week of classes as a student, she rode out to the country on a mule, preparing for a week of teaching at a one-room schoolhouse. It was arranged that during one week she would live with the parents of one student, the next with the parents of someone else.

On Friday afternoons she rode home and spent the weekend cooking, cleaning, and washing and ironing for her family. At first Grandmother Peggy came to stay with the children during the week. Soon it became too much for her health, so Ida found someone else to care for them.

Somehow Ida managed to keep this schedule for approximately one year. Then her father's sister, Fannie, invited her to come to Memphis and stay with her. Aunt Fannie had been widowed during the epidemic and would look after Annie and Lily, along with her own three little girls, while Ida worked. Aunt Belle, her mother's sister, volunteered to care for Eugenia and put the boys to work on her farm. Reluctantly, Ida agreed. She had kept her family together for a while, but now it was time to accept the help of other family members. This chapter of her life ended as she packed up their belongings, and the Wells family left Holly Springs for the last time.

Ida found a teaching job in the community of Woodstock, Tennessee, ten miles outside the city of Memphis. Now, she commuted by train instead of by mule. During summer vacations, she studied at Fisk University and Lemoyne Institute in Memphis, hoping to pass the examination to become a city schoolteacher and earn more money.

Life improved for Ida as she met other young black men and women who were eager to better themselves through education and job opportunities. At church, she listened for the first time to the words of militant preachers of her own race. She attended concerts, plays, and church and social gatherings, always writing her reactions to these events in her diary. Ida, now a lovely young woman, was a popular member of the community's black elite, though always serious and very proper in her manners. Once, when a young man tried to kiss her, she told her diary that she felt so humiliated "she could not look anyone in the face."[3]

As she studied and enjoyed many social occasions, she also yearned to do more with her life. She thought of writing a novel and put down notes on a subject. After taking elocution lessons and performing Lady Macbeth's sleepwalking scene at local affairs, she also dreamed of becoming an actress. More and more, she confided to her diary her hopes and dreams for the future, her uncertainty about the present. As she continued to study and become more exposed to the ideas in her books and of similar people whom she met, Ida's intellectual curiosity and concern for others expanded. So did her diary, in which she wrote endlessly. Writing seemed to be a craft in which she felt much at home.

If Ida's struggle for a better quality of life seemed to move easily, without a ripple to mar the surface of her existence, it was not the case with most blacks in the country. Although the government had passed a Civil Rights Act in 1875, outlawing segregation in the nation,

26

the guarantees of these rights were evaporating quickly. After the withdrawal of Federal troops from the South, conditions worsened. The African-American farmer was being robbed by the sharecropping system. Payment was in scrip, money good only at the plantation-owned store, where outrageous prices were charged. During the 1880s, many blacks lost or gave up their franchise because of force or threat.

As more and more of the court system and government in the South returned to the control of white supremacists, exploitation of blacks grew rampant. Lynching awaited any black who dared stand up for his rights. Finally, in October 1883, the Supreme Court declared the Civil Rights Act of 1875 unconstitutional. It was a death knell being sounded for the rights of all individuals, regardless of color.

"The colored people of the United States feel as if they have been baptized in ice water,"[4] wrote Thomas Fortune, a well-known journalist of the time.

Six months later, on May 4, 1884, Ida boarded the train as usual, to go to Woodstock for another day of teaching. She sat where she had always sat—in the first-class car called the ladies' coach—and began to read. Soon the conductor came by for her ticket but abruptly told her he couldn't accept it in this car. She would have to move ahead to the car reserved for blacks and smokers. Ida refused to move.

The conductor became angry and tried to drag her from her seat, but she promptly bit him. He left to get help and returned with two more men. It took the combined efforts of all three to drag her from the car, with the encouragement of the white women in the coach and white men who'd heard the commotion and come to look. The conductor and his helpers were applauded for their bravery.

At the first stop, Ida chose to leave the train rather than sit in the segregated car. Although she was somewhat bruised and her linen duster was torn and dirtied, she was not physically injured. It was the mental abuse which left deep scars, however, and she was determined that her voice of protest be heard.

When the Supreme Court declared the Civil Rights Act of 1875 unconstitutional in 1883, it had advised blacks to turn to state courts for assistance. This Ida now did. She hired a lawyer and sued the railroad for damages. Tried before a Judge J. O. Pierce, who had been a Union officer during the Civil War, Ida won her case and was awarded five hundred dollars in damages.

It did not go unnoticed. On December 25, 1884, the headline in the *Memphis Daily Appeal* read "A Darky Damsel Obtains a Verdict for Damages Against the Chesapeake & Ohio Railroad—What It Can Cost to Put a Colored School Teacher in a Smoking Car—Verdict for $500."[5]

The railroad soon appealed the decision to the state supreme court, and it was reversed. The ruling stated that "her persistence was not in good faith to obtain a comfortable seat for the short ride."[6] Now, Ida had to pay court costs as well as return the damages. Although she lost the legal battle in court, she had won an unexpected victory. Asked to write about her experiences for *The Living Way*, a black church weekly publication, Ida composed a spirited account of the trial and its outcome. Her article was so favorably received that the editor of the weekly asked for more. Out of this defeat, her life work began.

3
A TRUE VOCATION AT LAST

The editor of *The Living Way* asked Ida to contribute articles on a continuing basis. Soon she began to write a regular column under the by-line of *Iola*. Although she was somewhat concerned because she'd had no formal training as a writer, Wells undertook the job without hesitation, feeling she had learned something about the craft from reading extensively. As a child and a teenager, she had devoured all the fiction in the Sunday School library as well as at Rust College. Charles Dickens was a favorite, and so were Louisa May Alcott, Charlotte Brontë, and William Shakespeare. She had read little about her own race, simply because there was hardly any literature available except *Uncle Tom's Cabin*. She never mentioned if she had read it.

After Ida moved to Memphis, she participated in a teacher's lyceum, or educational institution, which met each Friday afternoon. Essays, lectures, recitations, and music provided her with additional exposure to good writing. However, she didn't plan to use a highly literary style for her columns, feeling it was not appropriate.

Later, in her autobiography, she said, "I wrote in a plain, common-sense way on the things which concerned our people. Knowing that their education was limited, I never used a word of two syllables where one would serve the purpose."[1]

This idea was based on her own experiences, even at such a young age. "I had observed and thought much about the conditions I had seen in the country schools and churches." She continued, "I had an instinctive feeling that people who had little or no school training should have something coming into their homes which dealt with their problems in a simple, helpful way."[2]

Her early columns were filled with local news at first. There were announcements of births and deaths, and reports on concerts, plays, and club meetings. Soon, though, she began to report on political issues, dealing with them in her straightforward manner that met everything head on, without compromise. Soon readers of both sexes sought out her columns, the men for the national and political subjects and the women whom "she [met] around the fireside."[3] Other editors enlisted her, and soon she was contributing to major black newspapers all over the country.

Blacks had been publishing newspapers as early as 1827, but most of these ventures soon folded for the usual reasons of no financial backing and few readers. Efforts continued, however, and the Afro-American press, as it was then called, prevailed. Newspapers such as *Colored American, Elevator, People's Press*, and *Genius of Freedom* kept the movement alive.

The close of the Civil War marked a new era in black journalism. It was felt that now, more than ever, black newspapers were needed in the South, to help in the education of freed men and women. From 1866 on, Afro-American newspapers were published in nearly every state at one time or another. By 1890 there were at least 154 weekly newspapers published for, by, and about black citizens. Most of them had mottos such as "He who would be free, himself must strike the blow."[4] This was the guiding principle of *The Pacific Appeal*, one of the earliest black newspapers, and could probably be applied to any or all of them.

In the summer of 1886, Ida Wells traveled to Topeka, Kansas, for a teachers' convention. She had been a city schoolteacher since the fall of 1884 and earned a little more money teaching in town than she had in the country. Finally, she could take advantage of the railroad's excursion fares to travel and broaden her experiences.

After Kansas, she went to Visalia, California, to visit Aunt Fannie and her sisters, who had moved there two years previously. Aunt Fannie had found better wages in this small California town, but she was lonely and begged Ida to stay. Reluctantly, Ida agreed, and she found a job teaching the town's eighteen black children in a run-down building with few provisions. Four days later, she resigned. She realized she could not remain isolated from the stimulating, intellectual society she'd left in Tennessee. Although Aunt Fannie implored her to remain, Ida left, taking her sister, Lily, now eleven, back to Memphis with her.

During this time, Wells had continued to write her column in *The Living Way*, as well as for some of the best and most respected black newspapers in the country, such as the *Detroit Plaindealer*, the *Indianapolis Freeman*, and the *Little Rock Sun*. She also contributed columns to monthly magazines published by the Baptist and African Methodist church denominations.

Black women were not new to journalism. The occupation had been pioneered by a woman named Mary Ann Cady, who during the 1850s founded *The Provincial Freeman*, a newspaper for black refugees living in Canada. She was considered one of the best editors in the country, "even if she did wear petticoats,"[5] and served as an inspiration for young black women who were Ida's contemporaries.

By the 1880s more than a dozen black women were prominent in the journalism field, but none of them wrote with the feisty zeal of Ida Wells. Instead, their styles were described as "poetic," "graceful," sensible," and "logical," and they devoted themselves primarily to the society and children's pages, or the religious and women's sections. A few dared to write about the lack of women's suffrage but were criticized for it.

Now, as Wells became better known for making inroads against racism, she encountered a new enemy: sexism. Although her boldness with the pen was admired by her peers, Ida's physical appearance never went unnoticed by the male journalists who saw and heard her speak. To them, she was never simply a journalist, but always a woman journalist, or "editress." The *Washington Bee* described her as "about four and a half feet high and tolerably well proportioned."[6] An editor at the *Indianapolis Freeman* said, "Iola makes the mistake of trying to be pretty as well as smart. She should remember that beauty and genius are not always companions."[7]

In 1887, Ida turned twenty-five. To her diary she confided her fears and frustrations as she contemplated this milestone. Many of her friends were married or soon would be. They were starting their own families, building their own homes. Suddenly, she realized that she was the only female teacher left in her school who was unmarried. This distressed her. Although she had gentleman callers, she seemed to be too serious and argumentative for a lasting relationship with them. Often, she sent them away. Even in trying to build friendships with other women, she quickly found herself disinterested in their conversations about home and children. Ida felt restless and lonely as she wondered about her future.

And now teaching began to leave something to be

desired. In all her years in the classroom, she had never taught higher than the fourth grade, and, suddenly, even this began to bore her. No wonder that for stimulation and gratification, she turned more and more to her writing career and the voluminous correspondence she enjoyed as a result.

Wells kept her teaching job because it paid the bills. From her writing, she received nothing except free copies of the publications, plus subscriptions. Nevertheless, her name was becoming known, and now people such as Reverend William J. Simmons pursued her. He was president of the state university of Louisville, Kentucky, president of the American Baptist Convention, and editor of the Negro Press Association. He called on Wells to ask her to become a correspondent for the American Baptist Home Missionary Society. For her efforts she would be paid one dollar a week. It was the first time Ida had been offered financial compensation for her writing, and she accepted quickly.

When the press association met in Louisville later that year, Simmons asked Ida to attend. Because she was the first woman representative, she received much attention from the other members and was elected secretary as well. Soon she was being called the "Princess of the Press."[8]

Two years later, on March 4, 1889, Ida Wells went to Washington, D.C., as the representative of the Baptist newspaper to attend the National Press Association meeting. There she met distinguished writers and publishers Frederick Douglass and T. Thomas Fortune, who impressed her greatly and were equally impressed by her.

Thomas Fortune was one of the most outstanding journalists in the country, and his *New York Age* had been acclaimed by both the black and white publishing worlds. Described as brilliant and aggressive by his peers, he even had once held a position on the white editorial staff of the *New York Evening Sun* at a time

33

when this was a rare exception. It was said of him that "he never writes anything unless he makes someone wince."[9] Fortune had this to say about Wells:

She has become famous as one of the few of our women who handles a goose quill with diamond point as handily as any of us men. If Iola was a man she would be a humming Independent in politics. She has plenty of nerve, she is smart as a steel trap, and she has no sympathy with humbug.[10]

Back in Memphis, Ida was invited to write for the Memphis *Free Speech and Headlight*, owned by Reverend Nightingale, pastor of the largest Baptist church in town, and J. L. Fleming, who was the newspaper's business manager. She quickly accepted. She now had a new ambition: to become a newspaper owner and publisher. Her demand to become a one-third owner of the *Free Speech* was accepted by the two men, and she managed to find the money to buy into the partnership.

The writing and publishing of the *Free Speech* moved along briskly, although Ida must have been extremely busy because she was still teaching. Life was not easy in another way, since Wells's editorials were critical of both blacks and whites, making her in turn the object of much criticism. But she wrote without fear of personal consequences. In one editorial she denounced a black minister who was having an affair with a woman in his congregation. African-American ministers in town protested this exposure to such an extent that Reverend Nightingale eventually withdrew from active participation in the newspaper.

At this time Southern states were in the process of disenfranchising blacks by any method possible, taking care not to disqualify certain whites as well. The method most popular with white supremacists was the "Grandfather Clause." It gave the vote to any male who

34

had served in the military or to those who had voted before 1867, and to their descendants.

In 1890 the state of Mississippi convened its Constitutional Convention and adopted an "Understanding Clause" into their state constitution. The clause said that any citizen who could understand a section of the U.S. Constitution when it was read to him was eligible to vote. White men selected those portions of the Constitution read for blacks' understanding and saw to it that they failed the test. Only the simplest sections were chosen for prospective white voters. Ida thought this unfair and outrageous and didn't hesitate to say so in the *Free Speech*, also criticizing the one black at the Convention who voted for the "Understanding Clause."

Next Wells took on the poor quality of education for black children in Memphis. She called attention to inadequate buildings, few supplies and books, and poorly trained teachers. Her editorials met with storms of protest from the board of education as well as from the white citizens in town. When the time came for election of teachers that fall, she was not rehired and not informed until it was much too late to find employment elsewhere. Even blacks criticized her this time, saying that she shouldn't have published the editorials knowing she could be fired. It was then Ida realized that she could not even count on support from members of her own race.

She spent the summer traveling in the Mississippi Valley area, increasing circulation for the *Free Speech*. Traveling as far as Arkansas and Mississippi and speaking to groups everywhere, she soon raised enough subscriptions to nearly equal her income as a teacher. Within nine months, circulation increased by two thousand subscriptions. She felt that she had found her true vocation at last.

Wells's newspaper was also sold by news dealers,

35

who quickly realized that many blacks could not read it. Soon the news dealers were giving them copies of the *Police Gazette* instead of the *Free Speech*. After Ida discovered this, she began to print the *Free Speech* on pink paper so that illiterate blacks would recognize the newspaper and demand the right one.

Ida Wells was in Natchez, Mississippi, in March 1892, when she heard about the lynching of a dear friend in Memphis. Thomas Moss, Calvin McDowell, and Henry Stewart owned and operated a store called the People's Grocery in a section of town called the Curve, because it was near a bend in the trolley tracks. Tommie Moss and his wife, Betty, were among Ida's closest friends. She was godmother to their daughter, Maurine. Ida knew how hard Moss worked at his regular postman's job, and then clerked in the store at nights and on Sundays, keeping the books as well. The grocery had been doing so well that it was taking customers away from a white grocer across the street.

Upon returning to Memphis, Wells learned that the white grocer deliberately had picked quarrels with Moss and his partners. On Saturday night, March 5, at eleven o'clock, a group of armed men crossed the street to attack the People's Grocery. Since the Curve was outside the jurisdiction of the city police, the partners had been advised by an attorney that they could protect their own property. They were armed and fired at three of their attackers in the melee. When Moss and his partners learned they had wounded three deputies, dressed in civilian clothes, they surrendered immediately, thinking they could prove their innocence of intent to fire on officers of the law.

The Sunday newspapers reported that "Negro desperados" had shot the white men and that the People's Grocery was "a low dive where drinking and gambling were carried on."[11] All day on Sunday, the homes of blacks were invaded and men carried off to jail in the pretense of looking for the conspirators who had organized the "attack" on the white men.

On Sunday and Monday night, a group of black National Guardsmen called the Tennessee Rifles kept vigil around the jail, to make sure that nothing happened to the blacks inside. On Tuesday morning the newspapers reported that the wounded deputies would recover. Black citizens of Memphis breathed easier, believing the crisis was over. That night no one guarded the jail.

While Memphis slept, a group of hand-picked white men entered the jail and removed Thomas Moss, Calvin McDowell, and Henry Stewart. Loaded onto a switch engine of the railroad which ran directly behind the jail, the three men were taken a mile outside of town and shot to death.

Later that day a mob looted the People's Grocery and destroyed what they couldn't eat or steal. What was left would later be sold at auction by creditors.

It was the first lynching that had ever occurred in Memphis. Of it, Wells would tell audiences and later write in *Our Day*, "a feeling of horror...possessed every member of the race in Memphis when the truth dawned upon us that the protection of the law which we had so long enjoyed was no longer ours."[12]

She wrote an impassioned editorial in the newspaper about the loss of her friend. "There is only one thing left that we can do; save our money and leave a town which will neither protect our lives and property, nor give us a fair trial in the courts, but takes us out and murders us in cold blood when accused by white persons."[13]

The black citizens of Memphis responded to this editorial by following its advice. Entire church congregations left, neighborhoods emptied, businesses closed as hundreds moved to California, Arkansas, Kansas, and places up north. Betty Moss, the wife of Thomas, moved to Indiana after the birth of her second child. Within two months, six thousand blacks had left Memphis, creating an economic crisis for white businessmen.

Ida Wells was visited in her office by representatives of the railroad, who wanted her to use her influence to get black people to ride the streetcars again. But she refused, saying that as long as there had been no effort to learn who had lynched the three black men, the black community would continue to boycott the city and its services, and leave as quickly as they could.

Wells felt that the lynching of Moss and the others was not just the expression of isolated feelings but part of a larger plan to restore white supremacy everywhere in the South. Ida began to study the history of lynchings in the South and found that most of the men who had been lynched had been accused of the rape of white women as a pretext for the lynching, accusations which were false in the majority of the cases.

As Wells continued to interview and research, she realized she was walking a tightrope. Sex was a forbidden subject; to discuss it in a newspaper was sensationalism in the extreme. Yet she wouldn't quit and continued to editorialize, even as eight more black men in the South were lynched within a week's time. Her final editorial for the *Free Speech*, published on May 21 before she left on a trip to the East, concluded with:

> *Nobody in this section of the country believes the old threadbare lie that Negro men rape white women. If Southern white men are not careful, they will over-reach themselves and public sentiment will have a reaction. A conclusion will then be reached which will be very damaging to the moral reputation of their women.*[14]

Ida Wells then traveled to Philadelphia on a previously arranged trip. When she concluded her business there, she took the train to New York, arriving on May

26. Thomas Fortune met her and said, "We've been a long time getting you to New York, but now you're here, I'm afraid you'll have to stay."[15] She was puzzled until he showed her a copy of another Memphis newspaper, saying that Ida's obscene intimations had brought the outspoken writer to the outermost limits of public patience. A group of white citizens had gone to the *Free Speech* offices and destroyed everything in them. Her business associate had fled the city, and a watch had been posted on all incoming trains for her return. If Ida Wells set foot in Memphis again, she would be hanged in front of the courthouse.

4
SPEAKING OUT AT HOME AND ABROAD

Everything Ida Wells owned in Memphis had been destroyed by the mob that ruined her newspaper office and its equipment. Intellectually, however, she knew she still had the power of her pen, and friends who would soon come to her aid. Almost immediately Thomas Fortune and his partner, Jerome B. Peterson, offered Ida a one-fourth interest in the *New York Age* in return for her subscription list to the *Free Speech*, plus a salaried position as a weekly contributor to the *Age*. Ida Wells continued her war on lynching with a vengeance.

The dictionary defines lynching as death by mob action without legal sanction or due process of law. Although lynching was usually associated with hanging only, many victims were burned, dismembered, or shot to death.

Lynching began in the United States during the American Revolution, when it was used by colonists to punish "infamous importers," "Stamp Masters," and "informers."[1] The term was taken from the first lyncher of record, Colonel Charles Lynch of Virginia. He used it "against a lawless band of Tories and desperadoes, who infested the country at the base of the Blue Ridge."[2] The person appointed judge was called Squire Birch or Judge Lynch and set up his courtroom under a tree. There, he dispensed swift justice. Usually the culprit was found guilty, then tied to the tree under which the judge sat, lashed mercilessly, and expelled from the county.

Lynch law moved west with the frontier and was used when there was no formal civil or judicial government firmly established in the locale. By 1835 the victims were no longer just beaten severely—they were put to death. As the antislavery movement began, lynching also came into use in well-established areas to control abolitionists. Up until this time, lynching was utilized against whites as well as blacks. It had not developed as a part of slavery but was considered just another means of maintaining law and order for all.

During the post–Civil War period, however, white supremacists seized on lynching as a method of instilling fear in the hearts of all blacks. The threat of being lynched drove home the fact that accommodation to Jim Crow segregation practices was better than death. Statistics told the grim story. In the period from 1882 to 1886, 475 whites and 301 blacks were lynched; from 1887 to 1896, 548 whites would be lynched compared with 1,045 blacks.[3]

Others had spoken out against lynching prior to Ida Wells, most notably Frederick Douglass, long an outspoken black leader and renowned international champion of human rights. At a meeting in Washington, D. C., in April 1886, he told an audience, "Lynch law, violence and murder [existed] without the least show of federal interference or popular rebuke."[4] Others who spoke up were Thomas Fortune and Judge Albion W. Tourgee, a Northern white man who was an attorney and activist for human rights.

Now, however, it was Ida Wells's turn. Feeling that

she owed it to everyone to continue speaking freely and openly on the subject of lynching, she wrote a seven-column article which ran on the front page of the *New York Age* on June 25, 1892. Ten thousand copies were printed and circulated throughout the country, including one thousand of which were sold in Memphis. Signing herself EXILED for this article, she detailed it with names, dates, and places of lynchings, with direct quotes from Southern newspapers that left no doubt about the real reason for these atrocities. Although rape was the general charge against the victims, it was seldom proved; nevertheless, the charge of rape had "closed the heart, stifled the conscience, warped the judgment and hushed the voice of press and pulpit," she wrote. Then she went on, "even to the better class of Afro-Americans, the crime is so revolting that they have too often taken the white man's word and given lynch law neither the investigation nor condemnation it deserved."[5]

Although accolades for Ida Wells continued to pour in from the black periodicals of the day, the white press, except for a few instances, ignored her completely. Unknown to her, however, two prominent black women in New York, Victoria Earle Matthews and Maritcha Jones, were determined to help her spread the word about her antilynching crusade, perhaps even to resurrect her old newspaper, the *Free Speech*. They organized a cohesive coalition of 250 women and proposed to raise money for her through a testimonial called the "greatest demonstration ever attempted by race women for one of their own number."[6] Ida Wells accepted their proposal and, on the night of October 5, 1892, she stepped out onto the stage of Lyric Hall in New York to lecture to an enthusiastic, sellout crowd.

As she looked around, she saw her pen name, *Iola*, spelled out in electric lights at the back of the platform. The programs handed out to each member of the audience were replicas of the *Free Speech*. Then the event began. Speeches, resolutions, and music preceded Ida Wells's lecture.

Finally she rose to speak and suddenly was filled with emotions she couldn't control as she began to talk about her home and friends, especially Tommie and Betty Moss and the dreadful cases of lynching she'd discovered from her research. Tears streamed from her eyes as she continued telling her story. When she finished, her speech was greeted enthusiastically, though she felt mortified that she had given way to "an exhibition of weakness."[7] The women then presented her with five hundred dollars and a gold brooch designed in the shape of a pen. She would wear the brooch for the next twenty years. Wells banked the money and used it later to publish a pamphlet called *Southern Horrors*.

This meeting in Lyric Hall signified a time of change for all black women in the country. Frances Ellen Harper, an activist and writer of the day, had stated that the nineteenth century was helping woman to discover herself.[8] Now the facts were confirming the truth of that statement. For the first time a significant number of black women had used their resources to mount a forum and confront a racial issue which concerned them. Other black women were eager to do the same and invited Ida Wells to speak to them.

It was at this time that she developed the basic speech she would use during the rest of her crusade. She first addressed the motivations for lynching, expressing the idea that slavery had so conditioned Southern whites' minds against blacks that it had resulted in lawlessness. Second, she spoke about the suppression of truth, emphasizing that force and threats were used against anyone daring to speak the truth about lynching. Wells then criticized the political and legal institutions of the country, arguing that they did not protect blacks with their powers, but only whites. She then directed attention to public sentiment, stressing that only strong

43

public feelings against evil would swing public senti-ment against lynching.

For the next several months she traveled through the East, speaking on "Lynch Law in All Its Phases." She was the guest of outstanding black leaders of the day. They were taken with this pretty young woman; they recognized that she was quickly becoming the voice of protest and crusader for justice they had long needed. Even whites were beginning to listen as she addressed them in Boston.

Not all experiences were good ones for Ida. Mem-phis newspapers, calling her the "Saddle-Colored Saphira [sic],"[9] launched an all-out attack against her with libelous stories. She responded with her usual directness and wrote to Judge Tourgee to see if she had grounds for a lawsuit. He recommended to her a Chicago attorney named Ferdinand L. Barnett, with whom she began to correspond.

While she was in Washington, D. C., in February 1893 for a speaking engagement, the newspapers carried a story of a particularly gruesome lynching in Paris, Texas. The event was turned into a spectacle. School children had been given a holiday to witness the event, and railroads ran excursion trains to bring in people from the area surrounding Paris in order to watch. Then, the alleged rapist, Henry Smith, still protesting his inno-cence, was burned alive.

This story, as well as others about lynching, quickly reached Great Britain and the attention of two women activists. Isabelle Mayo and Catherine Impey were involved in a human rights movement to aid victims of the caste system in India. Miss Impey had attended one of Ida Wells's lectures while traveling in the United States. Now she recognized that this African-American woman would be just the zealous speaker needed to lec-ture in Great Britain about the appalling treatment of blacks in America.

44

The two women moved quickly to invite Wells to speak. They guaranteed her expenses and stressed that this would "provide an opportunity for airing this intolerable condition."[10]

It was perfect timing on two counts. First, Ida Wells felt she was reaching deaf ears in the United States. Only in Boston had the white press and audiences given her brief attention. Perhaps, she felt, in Great Britain her voice would be heard by all. She was right, for the 1890s were a period of far-reaching political and social reform in England. The British were projecting an attitude reminiscent of earlier decades when, in their country, it was fashionable to support black abolitionists such as Frederick Douglass. Ida Wells sailed on April 5, 1893.

In that time, a trip taken by a lone female, let alone an African-American, was a historical occasion. On that trip she found a traveling companion in another equally distinguished woman, Dr. Georgia Patton, who was heading to Africa to become a medical missionary. Ida Wells's diary for that first momentous trip records little else but her bouts of seasickness. "Fourth Day, Seasick still. Fifth day, Seasicker. Sixth Day, Seasickest."[11]

Sponsored by the Society for the Brotherhood of Man, Ida Wells toured Scotland first, then England, for about two months, giving approximately forty lectures. Probably the first black American woman to speak from a British platform, she received excellent press coverage. She hoped these lectures would sway public opinion in Great Britain, which would act as an impetus to molding public opinion at home.

Back in the United States, Wells hurried directly to Chicago, where the World's Columbian Exposition, popularly known as the Chicago World's Fair, was already in progress. Nations from all over the world had been invited to participate in this celebration honoring the 400th anniversary of Christopher Columbus's discovery of America. Every ethnic group in the United States was represented at the American exhibition—except the African-Americans. Blacks around the country had petitioned for the opportunity to participate in the Exposition, but officials were slow in responding. A newspaper, *The Conservator*, called the exhibition "White City."[12]

Ironically, one of the exhibitions was supervised by an African-American. As a government appointed minister to the small black republic of Haiti, Frederick Douglass had been asked by Haiti's president to mount its exhibition at the event. A visible, appealing figure, Douglass made himself available each day to those who wanted to meet and speak with him. Whites as well as blacks came to honor his presence.

Douglass had encouraged Wells to write a pamphlet reporting on the progress of blacks in America, to be distributed during the fair. While she had been in Great Britain, he had called on the black population of the United States to contribute money to aid in the publication of Ida Wells's pamphlet. There was little response to his appeal, and Douglass became discouraged about the project.

If Wells reflected his sentiments, characteristically, she didn't show it. She suggested they ask the church women of Chicago for assistance. From a series of meetings, the women raised the necessary five hundred dollars required to publish twenty thousand copies of the eighty-one-page document. It was titled *The Reason Why the Colored American Is Not in the World's Columbian Exposition*. As Ida wrote later in her autobiography, "It was a clear, plain statement of facts concerning the oppression put upon the colored people in this land of the free and home of the brave."[13]

Frederick Douglass wrote the introduction and asked others to help organize the material and its publication. One of the contributors was the attorney, Ferdinand L. Barnett. Born free and educated in the

46

North, Barnett received his law degree from Northwestern University in 1878. Thirteen years older than Ida, he was not only highly respected in his profession but was also publisher of *The Conservator*, Chicago's first black weekly newspaper. Tall and distinguished looking, with a droll sense of humor, he was a widower with two young sons. Now, as Ida and Ferdinand finally met and worked together, they began to grow increasingly fond of one another.

A direct outgrowth of the pamphlet's circulation during the last three months of the fair was an increased awareness and interest in the black race in America. Finally officials of the exposition came to Douglass, asking for his cooperation in arranging a Colored American Day on August 25.

Wells and several black associations disapproved of Douglass's acceptance. They felt this was a last-minute token to appease all blacks and that Douglass should not have agreed. Nonetheless, Douglass proceeded with the plan, without Ida's help. On Colored American Day, the aging leader gave a rousing oration, presenting the statement of conditions under which blacks lived in this country. It was enthusiastically received by everyone, and Douglass's increased popularity gave him celebrity status at the fair.

Wells soon recognized that, even though the opportunity to present their case had been last-minute, Douglass still seized it and used it to its advantage. She immediately apologized to him for her lack of insight. However, her attitude over this episode foreshadowed problems to come. Her inability to combine compromise with conviction became even more difficult for her as she grew more powerful in black activist circles.

5
DEVELOPING A RHETORIC

In 1893, the summer of the fair, Ida Wells took another step forward in her life as she began her work with women's clubs. Asked to speak to a group of Chicago women, she inspired them to form their own club, similar to those she had spoken to in the East and in England. The women responded with enthusiasm and elected her chairperson of their meetings. She agreed, but only if a highly respected black Chicagoan, Mrs. John Jones, would act as honorary chair. Mrs. Jones was a refined, genteel person who had little experience in politics, particularly in activism. However, Wells felt she was the ideal person to lend her name to this new group. The reason was John Jones.

John Jones was one of the country's wealthiest blacks. He had been born free in 1817 in North Carolina and moved to Chicago when he was twenty. As an apprenticed tailor, he taught himself to read and write, then established himself in business, becoming successful beyond his dreams. Now he used his wealth to fight for legal emancipation through the repeal of Illinois's

Black Laws, which prohibited African-Americans from voting or testifying in court. Jones later became the first black in the North to win the important post of county commissioner and, while in office, was instrumental in abolishing segregated schools in Chicago.

Ida Wells was well aware that the respect and renown he enjoyed could only help in the establishment of a club headed by his wife. Ida Wells promised to do the work if Mrs. Jones would become titular head. Mrs. Jones accepted.

Out of this grew the Ida B. Wells Woman's Club, organized for "civic and social betterment."[1] One of its earliest projects was to raise money to prosecute a policeman for killing an innocent black man. It continued its work by establishing the first black orchestra in the city and the first kindergarten for black children. Later it became a charter member of the Cook County Women's Clubs, crossing the color line.

Ida decided to make her permanent home in Chicago and became a contributor to *The Conservator* while continuing her work with the woman's club. Another reason she may have chosen to remain in Chicago was her growing romantic interest in Ferdinand Barnett. Nor was she neglecting her work with anti-lynching organizations—she continued to lecture and to compile statistics and alleged causes on the crime of lynching in the United States, which she intended to have published in pamphlet form.

What may have compelled her to work even harder on this publication was the lynching of C. J. Miller in Bardwell, Kentucky, on July 7. Sent by the *Chicago Inter-Ocean* to investigate, Wells posed as the widow of Mr. Miller to interview those involved with the case. By the time she arrived and began her interviews, however, the lynchers already knew that they had killed the wrong man and that he had never been near the scene of the alleged crime. Her investigations indicated to her that this kind of mistake was happening too many times and that it was a clear case of scapegoat justice in order to "keep the nigger down."[2]

Meanwhile, an invitation came from the Society for the Brotherhood of Man asking Ida to return for another lecture tour of Great Britain. Before leaving Chicago, Ida Wells agreed to become the *Inter-Ocean*'s paid correspondent while on tour. The *Inter-Ocean* was one of the few white newspapers in the country which was sympathetic to the circumstances of African-American citizens.

Ida Wells sailed for England in February 1894, and began her series of lectures soon after she landed in Liverpool on March 1. First, however, she went to church to hear Reverend Charles F. Aked, who was considered the most influential and popular preacher in the city. The Society had felt it was important to have Reverend Aked's support in order for her lecture tour to be successful, but first wanted her to hear him speak.

She was very impressed and, at the close of the service, she met the young white pastor and his wife. They invited her to Sunday dinner, and from that moment on, the three began a warm friendship that would grow through the years. During Ida Wells's stay in Great Britain, their home became her headquarters. Through the Akeds, her relatives and friends in the United States could reach her if the need arose.

The second trip to Great Britain was far more successful than the first. Wells began by lecturing in Pembroke Chapel in Liverpool to an audience of more than twelve hundred. A reporter for the *Christian World* described her as "young, well educated, and a capital speaker."[3] She lectured a total of ten times in Liverpool, and the *New York Times*, through its British correspondent, reported that Ida Wells was "enlightening English minds on the subject of the lynching of Negroes in the South."[4] Liverpool newspapers and clergy were particularly impressed, especially Reverend R. A. Armstrong,

50

pastor of the Unitarian church. He was moved to write to the *Christian Register* of Boston, the Unitarian publication in the United States, to implore his American fellow Unitarians to "bestir" themselves and save their country from the evil of lynching.

Moving from Manchester to Bristol to Newcastle, Wells spoke in churches and chapels as well as in lecture halls, hoping that British religious leaders would awaken American churches to this crime. She began arousing support everywhere, and soon petitions were being signed by English Christians to communicate to Americans the horror they felt about lynching. The British press was even more enthusiastic about Wells and sympathetic to the cause. "I have quite lost count of the number of times I have been interviewed,"[5] Ida Wells wrote in a letter home.

Finally, she arrived in London but found little time for sightseeing. Instead she spoke at the Pioneer Club, the first woman's club established in London. As Ida Wells said in a report to *Inter-Ocean*, "It [the club] has outlived the days of ridicule, and most of the brainy women of London belong to it."[6] Before she left for home, Wells also spoke to sixteen members of Parliament and their wives at a breakfast. As guest of honor, she wryly told them that a gathering such as this to honor a colored woman could only happen in monarchial England. In democratic America it would be impossible.

The trip was not entirely without problems. Although she had been promised a salary of two pounds a week plus expenses, she seldom saw any of it and was forced to live on the generosity of friends plus monies raised at personal appearances. What little money she did receive was sent to her two sisters, Annie and Lily, who were attending school in California.

And then the Frances Willard problem arose. Frances Willard was president of the Women's Christian Temperance Union (W.C.T.U.), the most powerful women's organization in the United States. In addition, Willard was one of the most well-known women in the world. Four years earlier, she had toured the South as the guest of wealthy white people. Returning to New York, she was interviewed by the *New York Voice* for their October 23, 1890, issue. Willard spoke sympathetically of the white plight in the South. "I pity the southerners," she said. "The problem on their hands is immeasurable. The coloured race multiplies like the locusts of Egypt. The grog-shop is its center of power."[7] (Grog-shop was a name commonly used at that time for a tavern or saloon.)

Wells had reacted characteristically when she read this interview four years before. She printed her comments in her columns, and whenever she was asked where Frances Willard stood on lynching, she simply quoted from the *New York Voice* interview. It was Wells's contention that Willard had failed to denounce lynching because the members of the Southern branches of the W.C.T.U. might be offended. Later, in her pamphlet *A Red Record*, Wells would address the lack of support by Willard and the W.C.T.U., calling the words from the *New York Voice* "wholesale slander against the colored race and condonation of Southern white people's outrages"[8] against blacks.

Now, in the late spring of 1894, the two crusaders were in England at the same time. Willard was the guest of Lady Henry Somerset, a powerful activist for temperance in her own country. On May 9, at a meeting of the British Women's Temperance Association, Wells spoke briefly. Lady Somerset and Frances Willard were, of course, present. In her speech, Ida Wells criticized the white women of the South who had not spoken out against the guilt of their men in continuing the practice of lynching blacks.

When Wells was challenged about her interpretation of the position of the W.C.T.U. and its leader on the subject of lynching, she handed over a copy of the infamous *New York Voice* article, which was to be reprinted in a forthcoming issue of a British magazine called *Fraternity*. Lady Somerset learned of the pending publication and jumped into the controversy, sending word to Wells that if the article was published, she would see to it that the African-American woman never spoke in Great Britain again.

Fraternity magazine was sent to its subscribers a few weeks later with the article intact. Two weeks later, Willard was interviewed by Lady Somerset in the *Westminster Gazette*, in which they attempted to sway public sentiment against Ida Wells. The attempt failed and, in fact, backfired against Frances Willard. In the interview she admitted that the W.C.T.U. in the Southern states had no colored female members and that indeed she had blamed black illiterates for the defeat of prohibition in the South by speaking of "great dark-faced mobs whose rallying cry is better whiskey and more of it,"[9] in the *New York Voice* interview.

Meanwhile, the American press launched an assault on Wells, most likely in reaction to her popularity with the British papers. Those in her former hometown of Memphis were particularly vociferous. The *Memphis Scimitar* said that Ida B. Wells should be "tied to a stake on Main Street and branded with a hot iron."[10] The *Memphis Daily Commercial* devoted four columns of its May 26 newspaper to denouncing her, then flooded England with copies of that issue.

It shocked the British people into action to such a degree that a London Anti-Lynching Committee was quickly formed, with Queen Victoria's son-in-law, the Duke of Argyll, as chairman. Other British citizens who were powerful in their own right were members of this committee and thought seriously of sending a composite group of its members to the United States to study the problem.

Northern newspapers in the United States now joined the attack on Wells. The powerful *New York Times* printed the editorials of people enraged over the fact that such a group led by the Duke of Argyll could be influenced by a black woman. The *Times* went on to ask Southern governors to telegraph their opinions of "the English meddling in our affairs."[11]

As the attack continued and newspapers called Wells a "slanderous and nasty-minded mulatress,"[12] ever-increasing support came from the British public. The vindictiveness from her own country's newspapers served to confirm what she had been telling them. "It is idle for men to say that the conditions which Miss Wells describes do not exist."[13] said one British editor.

A success in a foreign country, a "mulatto refugee"[14] in her own, Ida booked passage for home in the summer of 1894. Home? Even she questioned that word. "I forgot that I have no home,"[15] she said. Then she must have remembered that she had some unfinished business in Chicago. She made that her destination.

6
"HOME" AGAIN

In early July 1894, Ida Wells sailed back to the United States, taking the longest route, via the gulf of Saint Lawrence, so that she would have more opportunity to rest after her strenuous trip abroad. During her four-month stay, she had delivered 102 speeches. As she rested, she must have remembered her newfound friends in Great Britain with much warmth and affection. The British press had defended her against two powerful white women, Frances Willard and Lady Henry Somerset, as well as against the white U.S. newspapers at home. She also had been treated with dignity at the many social events to which she'd been invited. As she said later in her autobiography, "It was such an absolutely new thing to be permitted for once to associate with human beings who pay tribute to what they believe one possesses in the way of qualities of mind and heart, rather than the color of the skin."[1]

The National Afro-American League, with Thomas Fortune as its president, held a massive rally for Wells at the Fleet Street African Methodist Episcopal Church in

55

New York City shortly after her return on July 24. Representatives of all the New York newspapers sent reporters to cover the event. At this meeting, Ida Wells rededicated herself to the antilynching movement for one more year. Through the newspaper stories which followed her appearance, the executive council of the league asked for contributions to an expense fund which would pay to send her on a lecture tour.

Three days after Ida Wells's appearance, an editorial was printed in the *New York Times*. A portion of it stated: "Immediately following the day of Miss Wells' return to the United States a Negro man assaulted a white woman in New York City 'for the purpose of lust and plunder.'" Then, it went on to say, "The circumstances of his fiendish crime may serve to convince the mulatress missionary that the promulgation in New York just now of her theory of Negro outrages is, to say the least, inopportune."[2]

Despite this snide editorial, unexpected reverberations from the support she had found in the British press and pulpit began to ripple through the American consciousness. Criticism of white American newspapers by their British peers and religious leaders had found its mark. The *Chicago Inter-Ocean* editorialized against "mob rule." The *Christian Register* endorsed the Liverpool Protest against discrimination, which came about as a result of Wells's lectures in that city.

Although newspapers such as the *Memphis Commercial* continued to harass Wells and referred to her speeches as "the mouthings of a wench,"[3] courageous and liberal editors elsewhere began to take a stand. Investigations and protests plus demands for punishments appeared in newspapers that heretofore had either ignored Ida Wells and her crusade, or vilified her. In the religious field the General Synod of the Reformed Church of America would issue a strong antilynching statement within the year.

Now Wells began to receive invitations to lecture, but there was an added dimension to these invitations. She would be paid a fee. In quick succession she spoke at the Academy of Music in Brooklyn, then went on to Plymouth Church, also in Brooklyn, and spoke from Henry Ward Beecher's pulpit. Reverend Beecher had been one of the most well-known clergymen of his day until his death in 1887. An emotional speaker, he had enjoyed great popularity through his sermons and writings, using them to attack slavery and to advocate women's suffrage. He was the brother of Harriet Beecher Stowe, the author of *Uncle Tom's Cabin*. This book was published in 1852 as a contribution to the abolitionist movement and became one of the most popular books of the nineteenth century.

The newspapers continued to chronicle Wells's anti-lynching crusade. After it was announced that she would be interviewed by a *New York Sun* journalist for publication on August 3, a group of black men called to ask her to "soft pedal" her accusations against white women and their relationships with black men. Wells refused.

When the *Sun* reporter arrived, Wells gave him the facts as she knew them. The interview created another furor after it was printed and was talked about even in Congress.

Then Wells moved quickly on to Philadelphia and spoke on the same platform with Frederick Douglass, her friend and mentor. She also addressed white audiences at churches and public functions, including meetings with groups of Methodist, Baptist, and Congregational ministers.

However, it was at a gathering of African Methodist Episcopal ministers that she encountered a problem. Thinking she was to receive an endorsement of appreciation for the work she had done, she probably felt relaxed and comfortable in a gathering of black religious leaders. Then a Reverend Dr. Embry stood up and objected to the resolution honoring Ida Wells. He stated that the organization should be careful about the young women they sanctioned when they knew little or nothing about them. A discussion of her qualifications followed, with an astonished Ida Wells listening.

Finally she rose to speak and told them that at every meeting of whites she'd attended since her arrival in Philadelphia, she had been greeted with applause and commendation. Now, suddenly, members of her own race questioned whether they could endorse her. Insulted, she told them she had done her work without their endorsement so far, and she would continue to do so. She marched out, smarting from the sexist treatment to which she'd been subjected again. Perhaps it hurt even more, coming from religious leaders whose support and understanding she'd expected.

She went home to Chicago, arriving on the 6th or 7th of August, to both a public and private welcome. The Ida B. Wells Woman's Club assisted in arranging a wonderful reception at the A.M.E. Church at Twenty-Fourth and Dearborn Streets. The *Inter-Ocean* reported that "This public testimonial was given to Miss Wells to show the high appreciation in which she is held for her invaluable service to her race and the unselfish character of her work. The large auditorium of Quinn Chapel was crowded to overflowing, and hundreds were unable to gain admittance."[4]

Then Ida Wells and Ferdinand Barnett made plans for the future. Sometime before her trip to Europe, they had reached an "understanding" that they would marry. Now she told him that she had dedicated herself to another year of crusading against lynching. Then she would be free to consider marriage.

She pursued the crusade in her nonstop fashion, crossing the country from California to New England and New York, then going as far south as St. Louis before touring Kansas and Nebraska. Each time she vis-

58

ited a city new to her, she would pause long enough to help organize antilynching societies before moving on.

During this time she completed her study of lynchings in the United States for the years 1892, 1893, and 1894. For many months, she had investigated every lynching she knew about. She pored over newspaper files, went to the actual scenes, and interviewed many eyewitnesses. In total she researched 728 lynchings which had taken place during the last ten years.

Published in 1895 and officially called *A Red Record: Tabulated Statistics and Alleged Causes of Lynchings in the United States*, the 100-page booklet was carefully documented, containing not only the statistical records but also a detailed history of the lynching of African-Americans and others since the Emancipation Proclamation in 1863.

In it Wells wrote: "It becomes the painful duty of the Negro to reproduce a record which shows that a large portion of the American people avow anarchy, condone murder and defy the contempt of civilization."

She goes on to say: "During the year 1894, there were 132 persons executed in the United States by due form of law, while in the same year, 197 persons were put to death by mobs who gave the victims no opportunity to make a lawful defense."[5]

Wells found that a third of the blacks who were lynched were accused of rape; far fewer were actually guilty of it. Other reasons for the murders were "incendiarism" (agitation), "race prejudice," "quarreling with whites," and "making threats."[6]

Even women and children were lynched. A thirteen-year-old girl named Mildrey Brown was hanged at Columbia, South Carolina, on circumstantial evidence that she'd poisoned a white baby.

As she investigated, Wells found evidence of many interracial liaisons. Not only did she print that relationships such as these did exist; she dared to say that many white women had initiated them. Black men were lynched for being "weak enough" to "accept" white women's favors, according to Ida Wells.

A double standard soon became apparent to her. White men could assault black women, but when white women had affairs with black men, it was called rape.

When she learned that the Women's Christian Temperance Union would meet in Cleveland, Ohio, in November, she traveled there, hoping to persuade the delegates to pass an antilynching resolution. Now Ida Wells and Frances Willard met face-to-face once again, but nothing changed between them. Later Wells wrote "that great Christian body which expressed itself in opposition to card playing, athletic sports and promiscuous dancing, protested against saloons [and] inveighed against tobacco, wholly ignored the seven millions of colored people whose plea was for a word of sympathy and support."[7]

Some months later Wells traveled to Rochester, New York, to lecture there and was invited to stay with Susan B. Anthony, the pioneer woman suffragist. Anthony was much older than Ida and tried to give her some advice, based on her years of experience. Although Wells admired Anthony and her work, she could not accept the older woman's advice to again "soft pedal" her printed accusations against the W.C.T.U. and, in particular, against Frances Willard. Anthony tried to persuade Wells that sometimes expediency was helpful in achieving one's goals, but Wells would have none of it.

Susan Anthony confessed that she had once used this means to extend the cause of women's suffrage. In 1848, when she had called the first convention of women to stand up for their civil rights, Anthony invited all men who felt as they did to attend also. Frederick Douglass was the only man who came. From that day on Douglass became an honorary member of the National Women's Suffrage Movement and spoke often at gatherings in the North. Yet, when the movement moved to the South, Anthony asked him not to attend the meetings, feeling that he would be subjected to humiliation. She also knew that his presence would offend white women whom she hoped to enlist in the cause. Anthony now asked Ida Wells if she had done the wrong thing, and Wells unhesitatingly said yes.

For her, there could be no equivocation. She continued to be direct with everyone she met. One day Mr. Slayton, owner of the Slayton Lyceum Bureau, approached Wells at the end of a lecture. He said that he would book speeches for her, as many as four a week, at fifty dollars each, provided she didn't mention lynching. That was an enormous sum of money. She was always short of cash, as monies guaranteed often failed to arrive. But she was unstinting in her resolve to carry this anti-lynching movement forward and refused to be persuaded by money.

In early February 1895, Ida Wells toured California and had completed a speaking engagement in San Francisco when she heard of the death of her old friend, Frederick Douglass. The loss moved her deeply, and she regretted that she was too far away to attend his funeral. Later, at a memorial in his honor, she said that "in the death of Frederick Douglass we lost the greatest man that the Negro race has ever produced on the American continent."[8]

Almost as if it were destined, Booker T. Washington rose to national prominence after Douglass's death. Washington was already well known. As principal of Tuskegee Institute in Alabama, however, he brought with him a different point of view regarding the problems of African-Americans. His words were conciliatory and soft-spoken, and he believed that only in compromise could blacks move slowly and cautiously into the mainstream of American life. Washington also believed that blacks as individuals should concentrate more on economic success and less on political advancement.

Many African-Americans disagreed, feeling that Washington's theory would only lead to strengthening the belief that blacks were inferior and could be treated unequally. Those in disagreement with Washington, Ida Wells among them, pointed out that the continued lynchings and additional segregation laws passed in the South were proof of this attitude.

Wells finished her year of dedication to the anti-lynching movement feeling tired and depressed. Although several white religious groups had passed resolutions denouncing lynchings, she felt that more could have been done. Exhausted from the traveling, the lecturing, and the attempts to mount a national antilynching organization, she felt "physically and financially bankrupt."[9] Now it was time for a giant step forward in her personal life.

Although Ida Wells had postponed her wedding three times due to pressing speaking engagements, she finally committed herself to marry Ferdinand Barnett on Thursday, June 27, 1895. She was thirty-three years old. Since she was too busy to make many of the arrangements, members of the Ida B. Wells Woman's Club took charge and planned a traditional wedding, complete with flower girl, orange blossoms, and *Lohengrin*'s "Wedding March."

On the evening of the wedding, as her bridal carriage pulled up to the doors of Bethel Church, she saw an overflowing crowd of well-wishers gathered on the sidewalk outside. Pushing through those who had come to share in her joy, she managed to get indoors. At eight o'clock she walked down the aisle to the altar, beautifully gowned in white satin. She was preceded by her two sisters, Annie and Lily, who acted as bridesmaids.

After the ceremony hundreds of the couple's friends gathered for a lively reception in the double front parlors at the home of Mrs. A. H. Brown, with whom Ida had lived. The wedding, considered a social event as well as a political one, was given much space in all the black newspapers of the day. It was thought to be the joining of two great hearts and minds for black equivalency, and was reported as such.

Although the wedding was a conventional one, the marriage was not and never would be, particularly for the nineteenth century. For years Ida Wells had dreamed of a home of her own, but had never shown much interest in domestic life. Now that she had a home at last, she found it supervised by her mother-in-law, who had taken over the care of her son and two grandsons after the death of Ferdinand's first wife. This bothered the new bride hardly at all. She found the arrangement to her liking and left it intact. After a three-day honeymoon, she hurried back to work on Monday morning.

Her destination was the office of *The Conservator*, the weekly newspaper she had purchased from her soon-to-be husband and his business associates shortly before her marriage. Now she had a newspaper again. Listed on the masthead as editor, publisher, and business manager was her birth name hyphenated with her new one: Ida B. Wells-Barnett.

Since the newspaper's inception by her husband in 1878, the weekly publication had concerned itself with the problem of African-Americans in political participation and social conditions in the local community. There was simply no straight reporting of the news. Involved in each story was the editor's point of view, a discussion, an interpretation, and comment. She had no plans to change anything.

An example of the treatment is this excerpt from a story originating in Clarksville, Tennessee. "The colored people of Clarksville were incensed over a multitude of wrongs. Not long ago, a colored man was lynched upon the charge of an attempt at outrage. An attempt, mind you. This is a comprehensive term in the South. It embraces a wink by a colored man at a white girl half a mile off. Such a crime is worthy of lynching, but a beastly attack upon a colored girl by a white man is only a wayward indiscretion. The colored people have stood such discriminations long enough."[10]

Although *The Conservator* labeled itself politically independent, it called the Republican party the champion of the oppressed and saw the Democratic party as on the side of the oppressor. Nevertheless all political candidates in Chicago were followed closely and, when a candidate (regardless of political affiliation) showed a fair and liberal attitude to black causes, he often was endorsed by *The Conservator*.

Echoes of color line and party politics reverberated in the columns of *The Conservator*. When a black Republican was the only one to lose on a slate of Republicans, the rest of whom were white, *The Conservator* turned on its readers, accusing them of being easily intimidated and afraid to vote for one of their own.

Ferdinand Barnett always had reflected the interest and the race consciousness of educated and public-minded African-Americans when addressing social conditions of the day. In particular, he was concerned with gambling halls and drinking saloons, which he felt were disruptive both in a moral and a financial sense to the average black man's life. In his paper he didn't hesitate to discuss how these unwholesome influences could be corrected. *The Conservator* stressed correct living through church and religious stories, with emphasis on home and family life. Under a column headed "Church Etiquette," the editor discussed bad manners and social laxities in great detail. Church service and attendance were characterized as "tests of a people's advancement."[11]

The overall tone of the rhetoric in the newspaper was characterized by a genuine desire to improve and advance the quality of African-American life. Generally, the stories reflected racial consciousness without emphasizing class distinction. Most of the time Barnett re-

Even as a child, Ida was exposed
to politics and racial problems as
she read to her father from
the newspaper.

IOLA'S LETTER.

Editor of the LIVING WAY;

The death Angle has flapped his black wings and among the number who went at his summons the past week was Mrs. Fred R. Hunt

The eulogy pronounce over her remains Sunday by Rev B. A. Imes and the large attendance at the funeral services show the estimation in which the deceased was held, and that society has lost a model of noble true womanhood and perfect ladyship; the church an earnest devoted christian, the husband a loving dutiful wife, who through all the vicissitudes of life, clung to and was true to him; and almost deified love by her sublime faith in him and hope of his ultimate reform. So patient, so uncomplaining, so gentle and kind, it would seem as if she could not be spared; that her childrens need, a brother's and husband's love, a desolated home—need her presence most. But a wise Father stilled the tired ____in, the aching heart, the weary feet. ____ the angel hands, now beckon ___ ____t for the loved ones behind ____ ____ Mr. Conrad Poole, a young ___ ____nic, a native of S. C. died here ____sday night Sept. 29th.

SOUTHERN HORRORS.

LYNCH LAW

IN ALL

ITS PHASES

Miss IDA B. WELLS,

Price,   Fifteen Cents.

THE NEW YORK AGE PRINT,
1892.

Above: cover of *Lynch Law in All Its Phases* pamphlet.
Left: this is one of the earliest-known published letters
by Ida B. Wells, printed in *The Living Way* on October 8,
1885. The newspaper was the first publication that
Wells wrote for, and seems to be typical of many of
the small black papers of the time.

RIDDLED.

The Mob's Summary Execution of the Three Negro Prisoners.

Taken to An Old Field and Filled With Shot.

Finding of Moss, McDowell and Stewart's Bodies.

Story of Their Capture and Punishment By the Masked Men.

Ferocious Resistance Offered the Mob By Calvin McDowell.

Wild Rumors Cause Citizens to Arm Themselves.

Unfounded Report of Negro Rioting at the Curve.

Mere Precautions Taken to Prevent An Outbreak—Judge DuBose Puts Gundealer Schuman In the Sweat-Box For Awhile—Exciting Scenes On the Street—All Quiet at Nightfall.

ALVIN M'DOW-ELL, Will Stewart and Tom Moss, three negroes implicated in the riot on the Curve on Saturday night, were forcibly taken from the jail early yesterday morning, dragged to an old brick

the noise of cars in the distance being the only sounds to disturb the workir.

Suddenly the bell above the door tinkled and hardly had its tintinnabulations ceased when a succession of resounding knocks on the heavy door caterar 'o.

"Who is that?" called O'Donnell, jumping from his chair and walking down the steps.

"We've got Hugh Williams, the last of the rioters at the Curve," came back the response. "We caught him out at Whitehaven."

"All right, wait a minute," said O'Donnell, and he came to unlock the gate.

As the jail gate creaked so familiarly, a man, with his face handkerchief into a disguise, slipped into the jail yard, and close behind pressed several others, disguised with handkerchiefs about their faces. O'Donnell's first impression was that the man...

oner. When he saw the masked men behind the supposed prisoner, he intuitively felt, he says, that something was wrong. He reached back to his hip for his revolver, but the disguised men caught his arm with:

"No, you don't. You keep still; we are not going to hurt you."

O'Donnell offered resistance, but it was of no avail. He tried to call the jailer, but the lynching party promptly stopped his outcry.

"We want Tom Moss, Shanks, McDowell and Stewart," the men next demanded, "and we want the keys."

O'Donnell refused to give them the keys, so they tied his arms with a small cotton rope, and searched him. The masked men could not find them, and the watchman even refused to tell them where they were. Three men kept watch over O'Donnell, while the rest of the party brushed past Seat and went into the jail.

The men tumbled things about in the various office rooms, hunting for the keys which were on a table in the main office. The keys were covered by a newspaper, and at first escaped the sight of the mob. Presently a man came upon them, and the crowd rushed to the cell apartment. In a jiffy the key was turned, the revolving door wheeled around, and in regular order, the men filed into the second tier of cells.

The prisoners were awakened by the noise, and many of the imprisoned negroes thought they were all to die. Through the small holes in the cell doors the masked men peeped and sought to find the men they were after. McDowell was the first one found, and he was dragged out into the corridor and put under guard. From door to door the search for the others was made, and in short order Tom Moss and Will Stewart were pulled out of their berths and grouped with McDowell in the corridors.

The mob then wanted Shanks, the negro who was wounded on the night of the riot. He could not be found in either of the first three tiers, and as the fourth tier is occupied by women, the mob did not think he was...

CALVIN M'DOWELL, IN LIFE.

the bayou, and then crossed over either by the ponton bridge or by the railroad trestle. It is a long walk through the railroad yards, and it is singular that the mob did not select some convenient place this side of the old water works point. Instead it went to the field on the other side of the plant.

A switchman in the Chesapeake & Ohio yards saw the party as it passed the old water works. One of the prisoners was bound by the hands and several of the men were pleading him with their guns. This was undoubtedly Stewart, whose hands were bound with a cord because he had so strenuously resisted the men.

Jack Pace, who lives near the field, says he heard about twenty shots, and they all sounded within a few minutes.

It is said that Car Inspector Walker, who lives at 262 Iowa avenue, saw the party returning from the killing. He did not notice the men closely at first, believing they were tramps who had jumped off an incoming train. After they came closer to him, he discovered that were masked and therefore said nothing to them. He only counted eight in this crowd, and it may be that the remainder came back to town by the Randolph road. Some time after they had gone, he walked up the track, and as it was daylight by this time, saw the bodies in the field.

At 6 o'clock in the morning Undertaker Jack Walsh was informed by telephone that the bodies were lying out in the field. His wagon was sent to the scene, and the driver and assistant put the bodies in pine coffins, bringing them to the stables near the Court House.

It was evident that McDowell had made a struggle, the wounds he received were evidently from a muzzle pressed close to his face. The faces of Moss and Stewart were less disfigured.

All day people straggled through the field to see the place of execution. The three pools of blood would not sink into the hard clay, and there they remained. There were a few stray bullets and shot in the clay about the spot where the men fell.

GAPING WOUNDS IN THEIR HEADS.

Bodies of the Negroes Present a Sickening Sight.

A large number of people saw the bodies at Undertaker Walsh's, but before noon they were taken to the undertaking establishment of B. F. Woodson & Co., at DeSoto and Union streets. A motley crowd of negroes ran behind the wagons and crowded about

SCENE OF THE SHOOTING

This cut represents the place where the shooting occurred, going from the city. The four black spots in the foreground there were that number, instead of three.

mmercial.

1892. **FIVE CENTS.**

The front page of *The Memphis Commercial* for March 10, 1892, reports—in sensationalistic style—the gruesome triple lynching of three black businessmen, which had occurred the day before. Wells would later charge the paper with playing a leading role in inciting the lynchings.

Holben, J. M.

ing verdict;
t were taken
by a masked
powered, and
to death by

HUMAN.

aler in the

alBose had re-
Schuman, the
s to the na-
ne day before,
or two cases
munition.
a court deputy
er for his ap-
Accordingly
DuBose said

that you have
ation to the
true or not

old some arms
ow at the time
atended to use
wed any to be

that you have
eople who use
have two cases
ayette county
s not forgotten
aracter."
selling to riot-

e stopped. If
more guns to
s closed and a

ten resolution,

are, close this
it"
e said: "And
I will hold

a menacing
ible for any-
ould do as it
who said:
in the sweat

surly manner,
could do as he

possessed any knowledge of their intentions.
The mob had come upon him unawares and
had tricked his deputy by a very credible
sage from the Curve, stating that an armed
sheriffs of other counties came to the jail
at all hours of the night with prisoners and
knock for admittance. So this was the best
ruse the mob could have chosen to gain admittance.

THE DAY AT THE CURVE.

Wild Rumors that Armed Men to the
scene.

About 10 o'clock yesterday morning
Sheriff McLendon received a telephone message from the Curve, stating that an armed
force of negroes, numbering two hundred or
more, were organizing to attack the white
people of the vicinity, and especially W. R.
Barrett, against whom they entertain the

TOM MOSS IN LIFE.

bitterest hatred. Other reports showed that
they were organizing at Cane Creek Church,
the principal rendezvous of the negroes.
Sheriff McLendon instantly ordered out a
posse of deputies to go to the scene of action.
President Clapp, who had also
received notice, gave orders for
a force of police and specials
to attend the Curve and protect the community if it should prove necessary.
In the meantime, H. B. White and Deputy
Sheriff Burke had brought the news of the
intended riot to Judge DuBose, and of a
threatened gathering on DeSoto street.
That dignitary, with his usual alacrity,
called Deputy Sheriff Perking and ordered
him to summon a posse of 150 men and go
to the scene of the disturbance at once.
And furthermore, if it was necessary, to use
any amount of force or weapons to quell the
insurrection. This force was speedily
raised and armed, and with
Sheriff McLendon at the head,
with an additional force, was soon
on its way to the Curve. Upon arriving
there they found no force of negroes, as they
had expected, nor any warlike indications.
Many vague rumors were afloat as to armed
bands congregating in the different locali-
ties, but upon investigation many of them
proved to be untrue. Immediately upon the
arrival of the force upon the grounds a
special force of thirty men had been sent to
the Cane Creek Church to investigate the report of the rising of the mob there, but if
the rioters had been there at all they had
dispersed. A few had been seen in the
vicinity carrying arms previous to that
hour. They had disappeared.
Later in the afternoon there was a report
that several negroes were parading that
part of McLemore avenue which is nearest
the Curve, but upon a search made they
could not be found. Near this place,
Deputy Sheriff J. F. Burke arrested Robert

were again rioting at the Curve, there was
a rush for the gun store. At Kupper-
schmidt's, on Main street, the store was
crowded, men buying revolvers, Winches-
ters and other firearms. Many of these
purchasers were special deputies.

Every car on the Desoto street line went
to the Curve loaded to the railing, but before noon the men began to return. Out
on Lauderdale street and kissimippi avenue men were hurrying along with Win-
chesters in their hands.

If at the broon any demonstration at the
Curve, there would have been a thousand
armed men out there within an hour. When
the news reached of the police force came in
at 10 o'clock yesterday evening the men
of several nations on the south
end floor of the Station House, and there
provided with cots to sleep on.
The police did not fear an outbreak, but
this report of a sensation in event of any
trouble during the day.

ONE OF THE COWARDLY NEGROES.

John Powell Sends Men Flying Down on
Alley.

A character of the threat made by the negroes was shown yesterday as Constable
John Powell was driving in the part of the
city where the riot occurred.
He was passing near Broadway and Hernando when a big negro standing on the
curbstone shouted:
"There goes one of the white-livered
——," using a name too vile for public
print. He made a threatening motion
toward his hip pocket, and Powell pulled
out his revolver and shot.
The negro broke and ran away when the
officer tried to capture him. A crowd of
negroes were painting a house near by at the
time. They scampered off the scaffolding like
cockroaches from a paste pot.

THEY WANT PEACE.

A Mass Meeting of White and Colored Citizens at the Curve.

Last night at 8 o'clock a mass meeting of
the citizens of the entire neighborhood of the
Curve was held at Scrape's drug store. Over
a hundred citizens were present.
The meeting was held for the purpose of
expressing the regret and indignation of the
community at the action of the mob Saturday night, and severe condemnation of the
grocshop of Barrett, together with other institutions of a similar character in the
neighborhood. The citizens were of the best
men in the neighborhood, and gave expression to sentiments which were manly, and
suggested measures which are adequate to
the necessities induced by the deplorable
state of circumstances existing in their
midst, and which, if they had been taken
practically earlier, would have prevented
bloodshed.
The meeting was called to order by Nathan
B. Camp, and Gen. A. J. Vaughn was voted
into the chair. The assembly was then addressed by Gen. Vaughn, Rev. Mr. Wear,
J. P. Jordan and others, who alike condemned Barrett's stir and the bloodshed in
their midst during the past week.
At a meeting of the citizens of the Fourteenth
District, held at the Curve on the Hernando
road this, March 9, 1892 it was resolved:
First, We call the attention of our county officers to the indiscriminate sale of liquor in this
neighborhood, accompanied by the paying of
craps and other games alike injurious to our citizens, both white and black, and without adequate police protection. We have for many
months viewed with alarm the coming storm, being sure the calamities now would be drawn out. The
granting of license to such dives as have infested
this neighborhood for many months is demoral-
izing to our citizens, death to real damage to our
property interests and rendering insecure the
lives of our wives and children.
Had the place kept by one Barrett not been allowed to exist, our families at least quiet would
now exist; our laws would have been upheld and
our country been saved the disgrace which now
rests upon her fair name.
Whereas, There are other places doing business here, also guilty of selling liquor without
licenses and in utter disregard to law and order in
the community, and tend, in all cases, tend to
evil and harm to our citizens, we very respect-

he C. & O. track
lood, of which

IDA B. WELLS ABROAD.

The Nemesis of Southern Lynchers Again in England.

WELCOME TO LIVERPOOL.

Why She Was Invited to Pembroke Chapel.

An English Clergyman's Recollection of What He Heard at the World's Fair.

LIVERPOOL, England, March 12.—*Special Correspondence.*—Directly after the burning alive of Henry Smith, at Paris, Texas, February, 1893, the writer received a letter inviting her to visit England and enlighten the natives on the lynching mania which seemed to prevail in the States. Needless to say I accepted the invitation with alacrity and within five days of its receipt sailed from New York. Ever since the suppression of my newspaper, the *Free Speech*, in Memphis, Tenn., in May, 1892, I had made unsuccessful attempts to be heard in the journals and on the platforms of the American people against lynching, which was fast becoming a national evil. When the way was opened in Great Britain I accepted gladly. Beginning in Aberdeen, Scotland, a tour was made throughout the largest cities of Scotland and England, and in each of these cities was established a "Society for the Recognition of the Brotherhood of Man." The members of this society subscribe to the following pledge: "I, the undersigned, promise to help in securing to every member of the human family freedom, equal opportunity, and brotherly consideration." Hundreds of names were enrolled at each meeting, and the strongest resolutions of condemnation and protest were passed after hearing my narration of the lynchings in the States. They felt it to be their duty to express in the strongest terms denunciation of the burning alive of human beings and the lawless wholesale hanging of the same. The leading newspapers of the United Kingdom gave excellent reports of the meetings, and many of them ringing and outspoken editorials against this state of affairs. The two months' tour closed, and I returned to the United States.

In Pembroke Chapel

The Society for the Recognition of the Brotherhood of Man, feeling that my first visit was not as thorough in its results as could be wished, invited me again this year to prosecute the work. I landed from the Germanic Friday last, and immediately received an invitation to address the congregation of Pembroke Chapel Sunday evening. The pastor, Rev. C. G. Aked, who is mine host, is one of the most advanced thinkers in the pulpit of today and has the largest nonconformist congregation outside of London. He had already chosen for his Sunday evening discourse the subject, "An Enemy of the People," and the discussion was devoted to Ibsen's drama of that name and the lessons to be deduced therefrom.

During Wells's second tour of Britain, she was a special correspondent for *The Daily Inter Ocean*. Eventually, she would send eight letters back to the Chicago-based paper—noting, as she would later state in her autobiography, that she "was in another country pleading for justice in her own." Here is a portion of her first letter.

The Daily Inter Ocean published the photograph, from
which this woodcut was made, accompanying Ida Wells's
report on the lynching of Charles J. Miller in Bardwell,
Kentucky, in 1893. The newspaper apologized for the
photo, saying that "in no other way (was) it possible
to give an adequate idea of the inhumanity of the
scene." The victim, as was true of so many others,
was later found to be innocent.

Booker T. Washington's philosophy of
accommodationism was in direct
opposition to Wells-Barnett's ideas.

As a young mother—Ida Wells-Barnett
and one of her children

Established 1878.

The Cous

One of the Oldest Col
the United

Published weekly

Ida B. Wells-Ba

The Conservator, one of Chicago's earliest black
newspapers, was cofounded by Ferdinand Barnett.
Writing to a friend two months after their wedding,
Ida confided, "I took charge of *The Conservator*
the fourth day after my marriage. I have been business
manager, editor, etc., all rolled into one ever since."

$2.00 Per Year.

rvator

d Journals in
ates.

2811 State St,
tt, Editor.

A RED RECORD.

Tabulated Statistics and Alleged Causes of

Lynchings in the United States,

1892–1893 1894.

Respectfully submitted to the Nineteenth Century civilization in " the Land of the Free and the Home of the Brave."

BY
Miss IDA B. WELLS,
128 Clark Street,
CHICAGO.

A Red Record (title page shown here) is considered to be one of the first and most important studies of lynch law and mob rule in the United States.

Ida Wells-Barnett and her children

Wells-Barnett was a champion of equal rights
for African-Americans and women, and was a
member of many organizations that
worked for these causes.

This stamp was issued in 1990 to honor Ida B. Wells-Barnett as part of the Black Heritage series.

Here, Ida wears the button that prompted a visit
by Secret Service agents. The buttons read
"In Memorial Martyred Negro Soldiers," and were
created to publicize a memorial service for
black soldiers who had been hanged.

flected his total identification with the black race by the use of the pronoun *our* when speaking of people or causes. *The Conservator* was a case of personal journalism at its best, yet most restrictive, form. Clearly, the newspaper had been someone's avocation, not vocation.

That was not the case when Ida Wells-Barnett became the paper's editor-in-chief.

7
A FAMILY OF
HER OWN

Ida Wells-Barnett's life became even busier after her marriage and return to full-time journalism, "her first and only love"[1] as editor of *The Conservator*. Considering the presidency of the Ida B. Wells Woman's Club and her many speaking engagements around town, it is easy to understand her feeling of being "utterly worn out."[2] So she declined an invitation from Josephine St. Pierre Ruffin, president of the Women's Era Club in Boston and prominent leader of civil rights issues, to attend a meeting there in July.

Probably she also was feeling the effects of her first pregnancy. Well ahead of her time in everything else, she had rejected advice about birth control from friends and had become pregnant immediately after her wedding.

The meeting of three thousand women had been organized specifically to protest a letter written to the British Anti-Lynching Committee by John W. Jacks, president of the Missouri Press Association. In the letter Mr. Jacks had libeled not only Ida Wells-Barnett, but all black women, by labeling them "prostitutes, thieves and liars."[3] A copy of the letter was sent to Josephine Ruffin, who then called the meeting.

The first National Conference of Colored Women met in July 1895 in Boston, at which Ellen Craft Crum, a delegate from the Woman's Club of Charleston, South Carolina, denounced the letter but also praised "the noble and truthful advocacy of Mrs. Ida B. Wells-Barnett, our noble 'Joanna of Arc.'"[4]

They stated that their goal was to concentrate "the dormant energies of the women of the Afro-American race into one broad band of sisterhood." Further, they would aid "all efforts for the upbuilding, ennobling and advancement of the race."[5] Out of this conference emerged an organization that came to be known as the National Association of Colored Women's Clubs.

Black women's power was on the move in the country. From the local clubs which sponsored Wells's appearance at Lyric Hall three years earlier, the movement had spread regionally. Now the libelous words of a Southern journalist had incited a national stirring. Black women were raising their voices nationwide and would not be ignored. Their agenda would address the issues of education, jobs, community service, and racial and gender discrimination.

Although they were advocates of women's rights, black women had never restricted themselves to the problems of gender discrimination only; they were also concerned with racial matters. Their earlier disagreement and eventual breakup with white feminists had resulted when the latter refused to support the Fifteenth Amendment, which gave the vote to black men before all women.

Black women were vitally interested in enfranchisement, however, and felt that only through the power of their votes could they effect change, particularly in the injustice of sexual abuse. Suffrage clubs grew all across the nation at this time as well. In some cities, more black women than white would eventually register to vote. Amendments giving women their franchise were introduced in Congress for more than forty years before the Nineteenth Amendment was finally passed in 1920. By that time black women represented the largest bloc of votes in some Southern states. South Carolina was one of them.

While Ida Wells was touring England the year before, her friend Reverend Charles Aked indicated that he would soon pay a visit to the United States. Ida hoped that he would arrive in time to officiate at her wedding, but he was not able to come until November, when he preached the Thanksgiving sermon at the University of Chicago chapel. Ida attended the service, and at its conclusion, Reverend Aked came down from the pulpit to greet her.

Reverend Aked and his wife had been invited to attend the football game between Chicago and the University of Michigan later that afternoon, but Mrs. Aked preferred not to go. Now Reverend Aked invited Ida Wells-Barnett to be his guest and to sit with the presidents of the two universities and their wives. She accepted at once.

Naturally she felt pleased to spend this unexpected time with her friend from England, but she realized that it also was an opportunity for them to give "a lesson in real democracy to our American friends."[6] She was the only black person sitting in the VIP section and, possibly, in the entire stadium.

If the presidents and their wives felt surprised or displeased, they did not display any visible signs of it, and the afternoon passed pleasantly.

During a conversation Reverend Aked suggested to Ida that it was possible white Americans were not totally to blame in their unfair assessment of blacks when their only contact with them may have been with the "menial class."[7] He further suggested that blacks should be seen at concerts, lectures, and other intellectual functions whenever possible, to show that an educated class of African-American existed. She agreed and had, in fact, felt this way for some time. It was good, however, to know that her friend from England shared her sentiment.

The Barnetts thought so highly of Reverend Aked that, when their first son was born on March 25, 1896, they named him Charles Aked Barnett. That summer Ida was appointed a delegate by the Ida B. Wells Woman's Club to attend a follow-up meeting of the one she'd missed in Boston. This year it was being held in Washington, D. C. Because she was breast-feeding her baby, she took him along, with a nurse to help care for him.

The meeting was historic, as several black women's organizations melded into one powerful National Association of Colored Women. Three generations were represented at the meeting, with older activists such as Frances E. W. Harper and Rosa Douglass-Sprague, daughter of Frederick Douglass, taking part. Others present were Victoria Earle Matthews, who had been one of the women instrumental in arranging the Lyric Hall meeting for Ida; Mrs. Booker T. Washington, just beginning her work in activist circles; and Mary Church Terrell, whom Ida considered to be "the most highly educated woman we had in the race."[8] Terrell was elected president, and Wells-Barnett chaired the resolutions committee. Also taking part were younger professional black women, representing the fields of medicine, social work, law, and education. The first female physicians in the South were black.

The celebrity of the conference was none of these women, however. That role was filled by Harriet Tubman, the elder stateswoman of women's activism and the legendary conductor on the Underground Railroad. Still a vigorous person at the age of seventy-six, she walked onto the speakers' platform to the cheers and applause of the crowd. Then, she held them spellbound as she spoke of her work as Union scout during the Civil War and sang a war song in a firm, clear voice. At the close of the conference, Tubman introduced baby Charles Barnett to the delegates, who officially named him "Baby of the Federation."[9]

By the time Wells-Barnett arrived home in September, political campaigns for national and state offices were underway. William McKinley was the Republican nominee for president. Although the Republicans had lost their power in the South, they still commanded many votes in the North and even took a cautious stand on civil rights by appointing a few blacks to federal jobs. Liberal Republicans, in particular, were pleased to accept black participation in politics.

The Women's State Republican Committee immediately asked Ida Wells-Barnett to join its speakers' bureau and go on tour. It would be a repeat performance of the previous year, except for one thing: Now she had baby Charles. Still, Wells-Barnett agreed to go, providing the committee would hire a nurse for Charles. Although she was going "to do my duty as mother toward my first-born and refused the suggestion not to nurse him,"[10] neither was she going to give up her civic and political activities. The baby went everywhere she did.

A nurse was arranged for each stop on Ida's itinerary, and she set off through the Illinois heartland, visiting towns such as Decatur, Bloomington, Springfield, and Quincy, handing over six-month-old Charles to a nurse during the time she spoke.

At only one lecture did the baby upstage her. One of the nurses was so eager to hear Wells-Barnett that she brought the baby to the lecture and sat on stage with him, thinking he would be happy and quiet as long as he could hear his mother. The baby was neither happy nor quiet and cried so loudly that the chairperson took him into the hall, allowing the nurse to stay to hear the speech. Later Wells-Barnett used this event in her speeches to suffragist audiences, telling them she was probably the only woman in the country who traveled with a nursing baby to make political speeches.

Before Charles was a year old, Ida became pregnant again, and a second son was born in November 1897. The Barnetts named him Herman Kohlsaat in honor of a friend who was one of their strongest supporters in civic activities. Now she realized she could not continue to be as politically active as she had been without sacrificing valuable time with her children. She "retired" by selling the newspaper and resigning from the presidency of the woman's club, after serving for five years.

She confessed that she had not looked forward to becoming a mother after marriage. She had been a surrogate mother to her brothers and sisters for so many years that she felt she had used up her maternal instinct. Now, with the birth of her own children, she found motherhood a pleasant surprise and, with her usual characteristic enthusiasm, devoted herself to her children's care. Also, Ferdinand Barnett had been appointed assistant state's attorney for Cook County after the recent election, and she may have felt there was enough politics in the family for now.

Conditions for which Wells-Barnett had fought were improving. A few white people of prominence, such as liberal editors, labor leaders, and churchpeople, had begun to denounce lynching publicly as well as to demand punishment for its instigators. Statistics showed an improvement, too, with numbers of lynchings down to 180 in 1895 from a peak year of 1892, when 235 people met death at the hands of a mob.

Lawmakers were slower to act, however. In August 1894 Congressman Henry William Blair from New Hampshire introduced a resolution to investigate all acts of violence, but it never moved out of committee wranglings despite efforts of the Afro-American League to expedite it through Congress.

State lawmakers were quicker to act, with six states—

71

five of them from the South—passing antilynching laws between 1893 and 1897. It seemed that some people had been influenced by Ida Wells-Barnett's crusade—although not everyone had, since lynchings continued.

In February 1898 a black Republican named Frazier B. Baker was appointed postmaster of Lake City, South Carolina. On the 21st of that month, a mob of three to four hundred set fire to his house. As his wife and four of his children ran outside, they were shot and severely wounded. Baker and an infant son were killed inside the home.

Since the man had been a federal employee, many people felt that the national government should intervene and punish the perpetrators. During a mass meeting in Chicago, money was raised to send Ida Wells-Barnett to Washington to officially denounce the brutal event. Her "retirement" had lasted only five months.

She went to the capital, accompanied by her five-month-old son, Herman. It was not a good time to be calling on congressmen or the president. The U.S. government was preparing to declare war on Spain, and that was uppermost in officials' minds.

The United States never had been happy with Spanish rule in Cuba. During a revolution there, many people died, and living conditions, economic hardships, and loss of civic rights grew intolerable. Rioting broke out as Cuban rebels and Spaniards fought to a standstill. In order to protect American citizens in Cuba from the rioters, an American warship, the *Maine*, was sent to the Havana harbor. On February 15, the ship exploded, and many Americans lost their lives.

President William McKinley sent notes to Spain, demanding full independence for Cuba. On April 19, Congress authorized the use of force to make Spain withdraw. Finally, on the 25th, the United States declared that a state of war existed with Spain.

Still, President McKinley greeted Wells-Barnett

and a delegation of Illinois congressmen politely, then listened as she told him that "nowhere in the civilized world save the United States do men go out in bands to hunt down, shoot, hang or burn to death a single individual."[11] While with the president, she also asked that national legislation be passed to outlaw lynching everywhere in the United States.

The president assured her and the delegates that everything was being done to bring the criminals in the Baker lynching to justice, that secret service agents were investigating the crime at that very moment. Eventually, eleven men were brought to trial in South Carolina but were freed by a hung jury, which could not reach a decision.

Ida Wells-Barnett stayed on in Washington for five weeks, hoping to influence congressmen to pass legislation which would financially compensate Mr. Baker's family for his death. But Congress had just declared war on Spain, and this commanded their complete attention. The compensation resolution failed to even get out of committee for a vote.

By the time she and baby Herman returned home in April, the Spanish-American War commanded the attention of everyone. Patriotic fervor ran high, causing dashing officers such as Lt. Colonel Theodore Roosevelt and his Rough Riders to become overnight heroes.

The nation had sided with Cuba in its struggle for independence from Spain. African-Americans, in particular, empathized with the cause since the island had a large black population. To show their support in a direct way, blacks attempted to enlist in the American army after the president called for volunteers. Many states refused them, and those who allowed African-Americans to enlist assigned them to labor battalions led by whites.

Both Ida and her husband, Ferdinand, demanded equal treatment for the black enlistees, insisting that they "fight not cook."[12] With other Chicagoans, they succeeded in mobilizing the Eighth Illinois Infantry, a regiment made up of black men and black officers, and a promise from the governor that the unit would be sent to Cuba to fight. When the regiment moved to Springfield in July for basic training, a ladies' auxiliary followed it. Wells-Barnett went, too, bringing little Charles and baby Herman. All the women cooked special food, supplied clothing and tobacco, and volunteered in the hospital until, true to the governor's word, the unit left for Cuba.

Later First Lieutenant John J. Pershing would say in his memoirs: "White regiments, black regiments...fought shoulder to shoulder, unmindful of race or color...and mindful only of their common duty as Americans."[13] Pershing became internationally famous when, in 1917, he was appointed general of the American armed forces in World War I.

In the fall of the year, Ida was invited by her old friend Thomas Fortune to attend an organizing conference in Rochester, New York. Fortune hoped to breathe new life into an old group, the Afro-American League, by giving it a new name, the National Afro-American Council, and renewed motivation. By now baby Herman was weaned and could be left with his grandmother, so Ida went without her boys. Once again, she was the house guest of Susan B. Anthony.

Wells-Barnett noticed soon after her arrival that Anthony addressed her as Mrs. Barnett, placing special emphasis on the word *Mrs*. Finally, she asked whether Anthony believed in marriage for women. The feminist replied that marriage was all right for certain women, "but not for women like you who had a special call for special work." Then she went on. "I know of no one in all this country better fitted to do the work you had in hand than yourself. Since you have gotten married, agitation seems practically to have ceased. Besides, you have a divided duty."[14]

Wells-Barnett knew it was true: She did have a

divided duty between family and public commitments. Nonetheless, when the nominating committee for the new organization put up her name for the position of secretary, she accepted without hesitation. Once more, Wells-Barnett was back in action on a national level.

8
DIVIDED DUTIES

Although Ida Wells-Barnett's ideas about a woman's role outside the home were extremely modern for her day, her ideas about rearing children were traditionally conservative. She believed that mothers should stay at home when their children were small, especially before they started school. Strict discipline should be administered, but with loving kindness. Good conduct was expected from her children even when she was not at home. When she was present, however, there was no question of poor conduct. One look from Ida Wells-Barnett brought her children's misbehavior to an immediate end.

Perhaps her thoughts about her divided duties between home and public life are best revealed by Thomas Fortune. Fortune described her as having "all of a women's tenderness in all that affects our common humanity, but she has also the courage of the great women of the past who believed that they could still be womanly while being more than ciphers in 'the world's broad field of battle.'"[1]

It was impossible for Wells-Barnett to remain focused on the world within the four walls of her home after she read President McKinley's message to Congress in November 1898. Not once did he mention the race riot which had taken place in Wilmington, North Carolina, on November 10. In that riot eleven African-Americans had been killed.

Thomas Fortune called a meeting of the National Afro-American Council in Washington, D. C., to condemn the president's failure to mention the riot. Although she was council secretary, she may not have attended the meeting. Many friends and associates did, however, and when it ended, a resolution had been passed condemning the president for his oversight.

Soon Wells-Barnett began to make arrangements for the first annual meeting of the council to be held August 16 to 19, 1899, in Chicago. Because she was so busy with her plans for the council meetings, Wells-Barnett didn't notice at first that plans were proceeding for the convention of the National Association of Colored Women to meet in Chicago at the same time, and no one had asked for her help.

Since her old acquaintance, Mary Church Terrell, completing her second term as president, was in charge of making the arrangements, Wells-Barnett felt puzzled that she had been left out. Terrell finally admitted that the local Chicago club women had indicated they would withdraw their assistance if Ida were included.

Wells-Barnett was angry at first, then deeply hurt as further explanation of this insulting attitude failed to be forthcoming. She had worked tirelessly to establish these women in club work, and now it seemed that they shunned her.

Finally, Jane Addams, a white social worker, provided an unexpected way for her to attend the conference for black women. Ten years earlier, Addams had established Hull House in Chicago, the first social settlement house in the United States. (A settlement house is located in an economically deprived area of a city where its staff provides educational, social, and cultural enrichments to the local underprivileged residents.) Addams was a pioneer in women's activism and was a prominent figure in international peace movements, women's suffrage, and social work in the United States. She would win the Nobel Prize for Peace in 1931.

Now Jane Addams read about the meetings of the black women's organization and called Wells-Barnett to extend an invitation to the officers of the association to have lunch with her at Hull House. The two women knew one another because of their pioneering work in their respective fields. So Ida Wells-Barnett went to the hall where the meetings were in session and stepped to the platform, not as a principal speaker, but simply to extend an invitation to lunch with Jane Addams. Despite the snub by her local club women, she conducted herself "as always" with proper decorum, hiding the deep hurt she expressed only later in her autobiography.

Ida Wells-Barnett displayed a lack of understanding as she began to experience a certain isolation from these groups with whom she had been so closely associated. Rather than examine her own actions, in which her passion for justice sometimes overrode her diplomatic skills, she just continued on her way. When she was left out of decision making, she was left to wonder why.

If her emotions and attention continued to be torn between home and public life, her course of action was not, even as she began to confront the emerging polarized factions of the black movement. Ida had always been militant, or aggressive, in her resolve and remained so now. It became apparent at the Afro-American Council meetings, however, that many blacks were becoming discouraged. They felt helpless as, more and more, segregation dominated their lives. After they heard about the North Carolina riots and subsequent lynchings, more

78

were willing to accept Booker T. Washington's philosophy of accommodationism.

But Wells-Barnett pursued her militant course, giving a rousing speech on "Mob Violence and Anarchy" to the assembled delegates of the council. In it she said, "If this gathering means anything, it means that we have at last come to a point where we must do something for ourselves and do it now."[2] Washington supporters branded her a hothead.

During the closing days of the convention, she was elected financial secretary. Now her opponents had a gender reason to remove her from their midst as well. *The Colored American*, a weekly newspaper, stated editorially: "It would be productive of a high degree of satisfaction to all concerned if the executive committee could arrange with Mrs. Barnett to take charge of a national auxiliary composed exclusively of women....The financial secretary of the Afro-American Council should be a man...."[3] Despite the opposition she faced, she kept the job for a year, then resigned to become the chairperson of the council's antilynching bureau.

Nineteen hundred was an election year, and President McKinley was reelected. Once more she campaigned for the Republican party with other prominent African-Americans, although Booker T. Washington was not one of them. When Washington became an adviser to the president, she was upset. She felt that he did not represent the majority of the blacks in the country.

In September 1901, McKinley died from an assassin's bullet, and Theodore Roosevelt was sworn into office. Washington remained as adviser, but no discernible difference occurred in the lives of blacks. By this time, however, she was expecting her third child and could not voice her protests in person when the Afro-American Council met in Philadelphia that summer. Soon after, her daughter Ida was born, and once again Wells-Barnett withdrew from public life.

She stayed at home now to enjoy her growing family. The Barnetts moved to a two-story brick house on Chicago's Rhodes Avenue and immediately encountered hostility as the first black family on the block. When her sons Charles and Herman were chased by white boys from the neighborhood, she ordered the white boys out of the yard, threatening to use force, if necessary. It was well known that she once had owned a gun during her days as editor of the *Free Speech* in Memphis. Whether she still had the gun no one knew, and no one wanted to find out.

Wells-Barnett loved spending time at home with her children. She sang bedtime songs to them, planned Halloween and birthday parties, and arranged for dancing and piano lessons, privileges she had missed as a child. She checked on their progress at school and was firm about the family's regular attendance at Sunday school and church. The only domestic topic she did not have firm ideas about was housework. Her husband enjoyed cooking, so she left the preparation of the evening meals to him. A relative or day worker attended to the cleaning and laundry.

Although she claimed to be retired, Ida Wells-Barnett could not be idle nor ignore civic and political activities around her. The dining room was her office, the table her desk as she wrote articles for newspapers and magazines. During this period, she produced a pamphlet titled *Mob Rule in New Orleans*, after a riot there.

Never one to back away from a fight with anyone, Wells-Barnett took on the powerful *Chicago Tribune* when it began publishing a series of articles on the benefits of segregated schools in the city. The articles were biased, with many interviews from white parents and educators but none from blacks. After the *Tribune* ignored a letter she wrote expressing her dissatisfaction, she went to the editorial offices to confront the editor directly. When offered little sympathy, Wells-Barnett realized she would have to enlist the aid of someone whose name would be respected by the *Tribune*.

She called Jane Addams, who quickly agreed to help. A group of white men and women were invited to Hull House to hear Wells-Barnett speak. Ministers, editors of other newspapers, attorneys, a judge, and a rabbi came. She appealed to their sense of fair play, asking them to assure the black children of Chicago an equal chance for a good education. Her words moved the listeners to form a committee, with Jane Addams as chairperson, to call on the *Tribune* and express their disapproval. Wells-Barnett was not present at the meeting, but its result gave her much satisfaction. The series of articles calling for separate school systems for black and white children ceased immediately.

In the winter of 1903, Wells-Barnett was asked by Celia Parker Wooley, a Unitarian minister, to help establish a center in which women of both races could meet and work together. She had decided to call it the Douglass Women's Club after Wells-Barnett's friend and mentor, Frederick Douglass. Ida agreed to help and immediately began to organize, although she was somewhat upset when Reverend Wooley suggested that a white woman be the first president and Ida become vice president.

Ida Wells-Barnett soon came to believe that racial discrimination of a very subtle sort existed within the organization. When Ida's name was suggested as the presidential nominee two years later, Reverend Wooley opposed it, although the name was enthusiastically received by the members when it was proposed. Ida Wells-Barnett declined to run and resigned from the group, announcing that she wanted to stay at home and tend to her new baby daughter, Alfreda, born in 1904.

Continuing to be involved with other civic matters, Ida helped the Pekin Theater become a place where black performers could appear in Chicago without discrimination, and black audiences could sit where they

81

chose and not in designated areas. She organized benefits to raise money for the theater, although she ran into opposition from black ministers of Chicago who denounced the theater as a "low dive." In her usual unflinching style, Wells-Barnett challenged the clergy to prove their accusations. Despite the criticism, the theater produced excellent entertainment, and many successful black actors and musicians credited the Pekin Theater for giving them a start with their careers.

When her husband, Ferdinand Barnett, ran for municipal judge, however, he was not supported by the black ministers of the city nor by their congregations and was defeated. She felt that if the black voters of the city had been encouraged by the black ministers to vote for him, he would have been elected since he was the only black candidate on a slate of twenty-seven.

Conditions for blacks during the first decade of the new century continued to deteriorate, particularly in the South as hostilities and segregation increased. In 1906 major riots broke out in Brownsville, Texas, and Atlanta, Georgia. By 1907 the South had passed laws mandating racial segregation on public transportation and in public places such as schools, hotels, restaurants, and theaters.

In addition, the "white primary" election practice had been adopted in most Southern states. It prevented blacks from voting in the Democratic party's primary elections by calling them "private affairs." The winners in the primaries were assured of victory in the general elections as well because the Republican party had ceased to be effective in the South and provided no opposition to the Democrats.

Discontent among blacks grew while bitterness and resentment festered in whites. This feeling gradually spread to Northern states, where riots between blacks and whites were occurring more frequently. In the summer of 1908, the nation was shocked by a particularly nasty riot that broke out in Springfield, Illinois, the city in which Abraham Lincoln had lived and was buried.

The riot began on August 14 as white mobs roamed through the city's small African-American district, burning property and attempting to interfere with firefighters. It took more than four thousand state militiamen two days to bring the riot to a halt. In that time, six blacks had been killed, and many wounded. Two thousand African-Americans left the city, many taking refuge in the militia camps.

The editorial pages of many Northern newspapers and periodicals screamed with outrage over the event. Oswald Garrison Villard, the editor of the *New York Evening Post*, was the grandson of William Lloyd Garrison, who had helped launch the abolitionist movement before the Civil War. Raised in the tradition of equal rights, Villard now spoke out from the editorials of the *Evening Post*, denouncing the riot.

The Independent, a liberal periodical, also lashed out from its editorial pages. Its editor said that, "Springfield will have to carry a heavier burden of shame than does Atlanta, for Illinois was never a slave state."[4]

Booker T. Washington, from his position as the most prominent African-American in the country, denounced lynching in a released statement, although he failed to mention the Springfield crimes. Other voices and newspapers in the North continued to criticize the incident but no definite action resulted.

In Chicago, as the riots still raged in Springfield, Ida Wells-Barnett walked to church on an August Sunday morning and she, too, wondered what could be done. When she arrived at church to teach Sunday school to a group of young men (ranging in age from eighteen to thirty), she put the question to them. After one suggested a meeting to discuss it further, she invited them to come to her house that afternoon.

Approximately one month later, an article written by William English Walling appeared in *The Independent*.

Walling came from a prominent, wealthy Southern family who once had owned slaves. He had become a writer, settlement house worker, and a socialist. With his wife, also an activist, Walling had gone to Springfield to investigate the riots. In his article, he blamed the local press for arousing a hostile public attitude against the blacks prior to the riot. He also condemned the common people who stood by during the attack and did nothing to protect the small black population of the city.

Walling was even more concerned with the political and business boycott which resulted from the riot. The boycott was an effort to drive the remaining blacks out of the city. If these attitudes became widespread in the North, Walling felt that political democracy would die.

"Who realizes the seriousness of the situation?" he asked in his article. "What large and powerful body of citizens is ready to come to (the Negro's) aid?"[5]

The answer to that question bothered most black citizens as well as concerned whites. What powerful body was there to help them? They had organized many groups, many times in the years since the Civil War ended, yet the riots and lynching went on. Had the Emancipation Proclamation been an empty promise?

In New York City Mary White Ovington, a social worker of independent means, was one of the people who read Walling's article. For many years she had worked to help blacks overcome the outrages of discrimination. Now, moved by Walling's strong words, she wrote to him immediately, suggesting they form an organization similar to the "powerful body of citizens" he wrote about.

It was not until January of 1909 that Ovington and Walling met. They invited Dr. Henry Moskowitz, a social worker assisting New York immigrants, to join them. It was decided that Villard of the *Evening Post* should be included in future meetings and that Lincoln's birthday would mark the beginning of a campaign to enlist support from a large number of citizens.

84

Villard drafted what became known as the Lincoln's birthday call, which was then sent to sixty citizens for endorsement, one third of whom were women (but of which only two were black). In Chicago, Jane Addams and Ida Wells-Barnett signed the document and looked forward to the conference to be held in New York City later in the year.

As Wells-Barnett traveled to New York in late May, she prepared her speech for the opening session of this conference with the hope that this new organization might become the powerful and influential association the Afro-American Council once promised to be. The name of this new group was now the National Negro Conference, although most of those involved were white. What could she say to this mix of educators, social workers, ministers, editors, and other dedicated citizens to inspire their hopes for a future free of discrimination?

The daytime sessions were scheduled to meet in Charity Organization Hall on Monday and Tuesday, May 31 and June 1, 1909. More than three hundred men and women gathered there to hear the speakers on Monday morning. William Hayes Ward, editor of *The Independent*, gave the keynote speech. In it, he said, "The purpose of this conference is to reemphasize...that equal justice should be done to man as man."[6]

Then it was Wells-Barnett's turn. First, keeping her emotions in check, she gave a factual report on the more than three thousand people who had been lynched in twenty-five years. Then, her voice filled with emotion, she asked, "Why is mob murder permitted by a Christian nation? What is the cause of this awful slaughter?"[7]

She had been asking these questions for more than a quarter of a century. She didn't expect to receive any answers now, but that didn't prevent her from continuing the quest for true emancipation for her race. Maybe this new organization could finally make that happen.

9
A MORE PERMANENT ORGANIZATION

Once the speeches ended at the first session of the National Negro Conference on May 31, 1909, the group began to plan for a course of affirmative action. Those who were militant in their ideas, as Ida Wells-Barnett and a few others were, feared that the program drawn up by this loosely organized group might not be powerful enough. She, in particular, wanted a strongly worded statement which would demand that congress make lynching a federal crime.

Despite a heated debate in the meeting which lasted well past midnight, the proposal to demand the outlawing of lynching failed to pass. Because most of those in attendance were white, Wells-Barnett may have felt this was a white attitude being forced upon the general assembly. During the meeting, it was reported that a woman (probably Ida) jumped to her feet and shouted, "They are betraying us again—these white friends of ours."[1]

Despite her feelings about betrayal, white friends came to Wells-Barnett's rescue when she was not nominated to a Committee of Forty whose duty would be to form a permanent organization. In trying to please everyone, the nominating committee had taken a moderate stance, selecting people who would not be controversial. Ida Wells-Barnett and other militants were ignored, and so were their philosophical opposites, Booker T. Washington and his followers.

Many of her white friends who had been nominated to the Committee of Forty offered to resign, to make room for her. One of them was Celia Parker Wooley, the Unitarian minister who had organized the Douglass Women's Club in Chicago and had caused Ida to resign from it. Wooley said that she had made a mistake similar to this (in excluding Ida) and didn't want to see that happen again.

Even though Ida Wells-Barnett's name was quickly added to the Committee of Forty, she was still upset over what she felt was a patronizing attitude of the organizers, and never really overcame this feeling during all her years with this organization.

Wells-Barnett returned to Chicago and her work with her Sunday school class of young men. She continued to lead discussions in church and at her home about the growing problems of blacks migrating to Chicago from the South.

In the fall of the year, another lynching took place in Illinois, this time in Cairo, far to the south of Chicago. A state law which was passed after the Springfield riots and lynchings of the previous summer now required the governor to suspend the sheriff of any county where a lynching had taken place. However, the sheriff of the county involved in the Cairo lynching asked to be reinstated to his former position. It looked as if his request would be granted unless someone opposed him.

Ferdinand Barnett, in his official capacity as assistant state's attorney, had worked on this case but had been unable to find any new evidence to present at the sheriff's reinstatement hearing. He came home from work to report his lack of progress and finished by telling his wife, "And so it would seem that you will have to go to Cairo and get the facts."[2] Because of his official position as assistant state's attorney, he could not go himself.

She was reluctant to go at first because she had been accused by some of her male associates of "jumping in ahead of them and doing work without giving them a chance."[3] She also wanted to stay home with her children, but it was one of them who changed her mind. All the children had been present when their father told of the problem. Now Charles, aged thirteen, came to his mother at bedtime and said, "Mother, if you don't go, nobody else will."[4]

She boarded the train the following morning for Cairo. There she spent three days visiting the scene and interviewing eyewitnesses before going to Springfield to the hearing.

The scene that awaited her in court appeared hopeless. The sheriff was accompanied by leading citizens, his priest, an attorney, a state senator, and stacks of letters of support.

Ida Wells-Barnett sat at the prosecutor's table, alone. Although she and her husband had thought the state's attorney general would present the case against reinstatement, the governor suddenly announced that "Mrs. Barnett is here to represent the colored people of Illinois."[5]

First, she read a legal paper prepared by her husband. Then, speaking for more than four hours, she presented the facts that she had found in Cairo. She concluded by asking the governor to reject the sheriff's reinstatement by saying, "it [the reinstatement] will mean an encouragement to mob violence."[6]

Based on her evidence, the governor concluded that the sheriff had acted illegally by not protecting his prisoner and had thus allowed the lynching to take place.

The sheriff was not reinstated, and there were no more lynchings in Illinois. It was a landmark case, and no one was more surprised than Ida Wells-Barnett at the fair, but unexpected, decision.

In May 1910, the National Negro Conference held its second annual meeting in New York, and Wells-Barnett traveled east to attend the sessions. She was probably showered with attention at that time. She had been told that the executive committee, of which she was a member, felt her work to prevent the reinstatement of the Illinois sheriff was "the most outstanding thing that had been done for the race during the year."[7]

It was during this series of meetings that the group organized a permanent association, and the name National Association for the Advancement of Colored People (NAACP) was decided upon. Dr. W.E.B. DuBois became director of publicity and research, the first paid officer of the organization.

Dr. DuBois, a socialist and historian, taught at Atlanta University and was highly regarded in academic circles. In 1895, he became the first black to receive a doctorate at Harvard. In addition he had studied and traveled in Europe and written two powerful books, *The Suppression of the African Slave-Trade to the United States* and *The Souls of Black Folk*.

DuBois disagreed with Booker T. Washington's philosophy, feeling that Washington's acceptance of racial segregation only strengthened white people's belief that blacks were inferior. DuBois agreed with Wells-Barnett that the continued lynchings of Negroes was strong evidence of whites' attitude of supremacy. In 1905 DuBois had founded an organized protest against discrimination called the Niagara Movement, named after the city in which the group met. DuBois and others in the movement received widespread support and acclaim from many black leaders and whites sympathetic to the cause. His leadership and academic standing undoubtedly contributed to his appointment now as the first paid official of the NAACP.

Once more, Ida Wells-Barnett returned to Chicago, to her family, her Sunday school class, and her concern about the growing black population. During the fifteen years since she had moved to the city, the black population had nearly tripled. Most of the newcomers had been farmers in the South and had little knowledge of city life and no place to turn for help after they arrived.

Black women quickly found work as domestics, but men found work less easily. Not only did they have little training for the few jobs that were available, but the labor unions discriminated against them, further hampering opportunities. In addition, they had no place to stay in the city because the YMCAs and hotels would not accept them. The only places African-American men were welcome were in saloons and gambling halls.

This was an intolerable situation, and Ida Wells-Barnett soon worked out a solution. With her Sunday school class's assistance, she organized the Negro Fellowship League. Soon the league opened a reading room and social center in the heart of the black ghetto where newcomers could find physical and financial help. She gave credit for her idea to Jane Addams's Hull House, which helped the many immigrants streaming into Chicago from European countries.

Again Ida Wells-Barnett set herself no easy task. Financial backing of the project was a problem from the beginning, and personnel was another. Although a secretary was hired and the young men of her Sunday school class volunteered to staff the center, Ida had to be present every day she was in Chicago. Fortunately, a white couple volunteered to help with the league's financial backing, guaranteeing the rent and the secretary's salary for the first three years.

The first floor of the center contained tables, chairs, a piano, games, and a selection of hometown newspapers.

90

The second floor was converted into a dormitory where young men could sleep for a few nights for a nominal fee. By the end of the first year, an average of forty to fifty persons a day came in to read or socialize or look for a job. One hundred fifteen young men found work through the center's employment office during this time.

The league helped blacks in other ways. Knowing that the police made life difficult for black male immigrants, often arresting them and sending them to prison for crimes they did not commit, she was ever alert to this discriminatory action. One day in August, she heard of a man named Steve Greene who had been arrested by the Chicago police. Held at the police station for four days without food or water while being questioned regarding a shooting in Arkansas, Greene became so ill that he was transferred to a hospital.

Wells-Barnett investigated and discovered that Greene had been shot three times by a former employer before he had defended himself and killed his assailant. Greene had escaped north, getting as far as Chicago before the police apprehended him. Now the state of Arkansas demanded his return—not to be tried fairly in the courts, however. It was known that he would be lynched when he was returned.

Wells-Barnett obtained a writ of habeas corpus and publicly offered one hundred dollars to any sheriff who would intercept those having custody of Greene and return him to Chicago, where he at least could be granted a fair hearing. Before he could be taken over the state line, Greene was returned to Chicago.

Much legal wrangling went on between the states of Illinois and Arkansas before the law once again determined that Greene should be returned to Arkansas. Before this happened, however, he was spirited out of Chicago and into Canada. Wells-Barnett was directly involved in his escape and later, when the Arkansas authorities dismissed charges, she welcomed Greene back to Chicago and the league center, through which he found work and a place to stay.

The NAACP continued to hold organizational meetings and called for another national conference to be held in New York City in December 1910. Dissension within the group continued to be a problem as the organization grew. Booker T. Washington once expressed the naive belief that his black friends could not work together in harmony and "in this respect, white people excell us very much."[8] Whether or not they worked harmoniously together, the members of the NAACP had been effective in this first full year of organization. Through the case *Quinn vs. the United States*, the association saw the Supreme Court declare the "grandfather clause" of state constitutions as an unconstitutional barrier to voting rights under the Fifteenth Amendment.

Wells-Barnett continued to have difficulties getting along with members of the NAACP, particularly when the Chicago branch of the organization called a meeting at Hull House without notifying her. Disregarding the fact that she was totally involved with the Negro Fellowship League and had little time or energy left for anything else, she complained about being left out of the NAACP's organizational activities. She thoroughly resented the fact that Jane Addams wanted to "mother" the event, as Ida expressed in her autobiography.

For a while, Wells-Barnett lent her militant voice to the Chicago branch of the NAACP—in direct opposition to the supporters of Booker T. Washington, who continued to believe the NAACP was too radical in its demands for equal rights. However, when the association decided to have its annual conference in Chicago in 1912 and Jane Addams was called the moving spirit of the event, Ida felt slighted. She criticized the meetings, saying there had been insufficient notice to prepare for them.

Much of her dissatisfaction undoubtedly came from her deepseated convictions that more must be done immediately to ensure the rights of her people. Her impatience and lack of diplomacy must have also reflected her weariness, as she worked night and day for her league. She was fifty years old now, an age when women of her era began to slow their activities and rest on past achievements.

Not Ida Wells-Barnett. When financial support of the league ended, she found a job as *probation officer*, with a salary of one hundred fifty dollars a month, which she turned over to the social center to carry on its activities. She became the first woman to be appointed to the position of probation officer in Chicago.

Her appointment meant that she now spent her days in the municipal courts working with parolees and her nights at the center helping the jobless and homeless. Her youngest child, Alfreda, stayed in touch with her mother with a daily telephone call at lunch time.

Somehow, during these years, Ida Wells-Barnett managed to keep up her political activities, particularly in women's suffrage. Even though she had never kept it a secret that she often distrusted whites, she worked best with white women in the suffrage movement. Since first coming to Chicago, she had been a member of the white-dominated Women's Suffrage Association.

In Illinois women could vote in local elections, although they still were not eligible to vote on a national level. Soon after this was established at the state level, Ida formed the Alpha Suffrage Club, the first such organization for black women in the state and, possibly, the country. Members went from door to door in the predominantly black Second Ward of Chicago, assisting women to register to vote, in an attempt to elect a black alderman (a member of a municipal body) to the city council. The women were criticized by men of their race, who told them to go home and take care of their families and not poke around into affairs that were none of their business. The women ignored the criticism and managed to get out the vote so successfully that, soon, politicians came to them, looking for their support. The following year a black alderman would be elected.

In 1912 Democrat Woodrow Wilson was elected president of the United States when Republicans split their votes between President William Howard Taft and former President Theodore Roosevelt. Wilson was the first Democrat to hold the office in twenty years. Ida Wells-Barnett's choice had been the incumbent Taft.

A few months later, shortly before Wilson's inauguration in March 1913, Ida Wells-Barnett was one of thousands of women who converged in Washington, D. C., to campaign for women's suffrage nationwide. A march up Pennsylvania Avenue was scheduled as the climax of this rally. Ida Wells-Barnett was asked by officers of the National American Woman Suffrage Association not to participate in the march because she might offend Southern white women. She ignored them and marched anyway, basking in the support of the Illinois delegation. One admirer wrote a rhyme about her, beginning:

Side by side with the whites she walked,
Step after step the Southerners balked,
But Illinois, fond of order and grace,
Stuck to the black Queen of our race.[9]

Black people voiced concern over Wilson's election since he was a Democrat who had been born and reared in the South. And in his first few months of office, he gave them something to be concerned about by appointing five Southerners to his cabinet. Soon those cabinet members had segregated their offices as well as forbidden blacks to use the restaurants and restrooms in their building.

On November 6, 1913, Ida Wells-Barnett returned to Washington, D. C., this time as a member of a delegation from the National Equal Rights League. Founded by William Monroe Trotter, who was the opposition voice to Booker T. Washington in national affairs, the league dedicated itself to being "of, for and led by the colored people."[10] Wells-Barnett and Trotter knew one another well from the founding days of the NAACP.

It was the duty of the delegation to meet with President Wilson and discuss the issue of segregation in his administration. During the meeting, Wells-Barnett and Trotter spoke for the group, reading a statement and presenting a petition. The president replied politely, and then they left, feeling their thirty-five-minute meeting had been productive. A year later nothing had changed, and Trotter asked for and received another appointment with the president.

On November 12, 1914, he and his delegation came to the White House once again. The president said that he had investigated and learned that "the segregation was caused by friction between colored and white clerks."[11] He went on to say, "Segregation is not humiliating but a benefit."[12] Naturally, Trotter was upset and continued to confront the president. But Wilson became irritated and broke off the conversation, calling Trotter offensive and refusing to meet with him again.

The next day the story of the confrontation was in the newspapers, and segregation became headline news once more. Wells-Barnett hadn't been present at the second meeting, but her own confrontation with the government would soon make headlines of its own.

10
A TIME OF
FRUSTRATION

During 1913 Ida continued to work as a probation officer and kept the center going, although it was always in need of additional funds. She also found the time to write and publish an article in *Survey* magazine titled "Our Country's Lynching Record." She was, first and foremost a working journalist.

When the Illinois legislature convened that year, Wells-Barnett was on hand as well. She was one of two or three hundred black women who protested in committee sessions against bills which were discriminatory. As a result of their protest, not one bill left the committee hearings. Some of the Democratic legislators were so impressed with these women that they told them they would set aside $25,000 to be used for a fiftieth anniversary observance of the Emancipation Proclamation. The governor then appointed a commission composed of three white men, one white woman, and four black men to oversee the spending of the money and arrange the observance. Not one black woman was appointed.

Ida Wells-Barnett had been scheduled to speak at a

breakfast meeting the morning she read about this oversight in the newspaper. Instead of giving her regular speech, she aroused the audience of black women to such indignation that they sent the governor a strong protest. Predictably, nothing was done.

Wells-Barnett continued to write and speak for a black woman representative on the committee. It was a frustrating time for her, and she admitted to being discouraged. Finally a place for a black woman became available when the lone white woman on the committee resigned, due to illness. The governor then appointed Dr. Mary Waring, an acquaintance of Ida Wells-Barnett. Ida insisted she had not wanted the appointment herself, but was disappointed that her work behind the scenes in getting a black woman placed on the commission was not recognized.

In 1914 World War I broke out in Europe, involving all the main European powers. Although the assassination of Archduke Francis Ferdinand of Austria-Hungary triggered the war, it ignited because of fierce nationalist feelings and pride among the major countries. France, Great Britain, and Russia were allied against Austria-Hungary and Germany. President Wilson vowed to keep the United States out of the conflict, but it was difficult when the German submarine fleet began to attack U.S. ships at sea. After the sinking of the *Lusitania* in 1915, in which more than one hundred American lives were lost, the United States experienced a steady slide toward involvement.

In 1916 it was time once again for a presidential election, and Woodrow Wilson was renominated by the Democratic party. He helped to shape the party's platform, or principles, which urged women's suffrage.

The Republicans also needed a statement in their platform to address the issue of women's suffrage. In June of that year, five thousand black and white women marched together down Michigan Avenue in Chicago, campaigning for an amendment to the Constitution that would grant women the right to vote and urging the Republicans to include suffrage in their platform. Ida Wells-Barnett led her group in this march. Alfreda marched with her mother, wearing a white dress decorated with streamers bearing the name *Alpha Suffrage Club*.

Wilson was reelected, and on April 2, 1917, he called a special session of Congress. In a speech to the members, he said, "the world must be made safe for democracy."[1] Congress agreed, declaring war on Germany on April 6.

But the United States was not prepared for war, either militarily, materially, or emotionally. Soon a draft of all men aged twenty-one through thirty was organized, later broadened to include men from eighteen to forty-five. More than 360,000 blacks, organized into all-black units, eventually would serve in the armed forces during World War I.

Government propaganda soon had the citizens convinced this war was being fought for liberty and democracy. Anyone who dared to criticize or oppose the war came under suspicion and could even be brought to trial under certain wartime laws. The emotional fever of public opinion sometimes overruled common sense.

Wells-Barnett and the Fellowship League worked hard in Chicago, raising funds so that candy and cigarettes could be distributed to black soldiers at Camp Grant, located near Chicago. In addition they soon began providing assistance with travel plans at the railroad station. Many blacks were traveling away from home for the first time now, as thousands from the South migrated North. Discrimination, police brutality, and lynchings in the South were a few of the reasons blacks moved north. Crop losses and insect pests on the farms were other persuaders. And now, because of the war, immigrant labor from Europe was no longer available. The resulting labor shortage in the North created a demand for the services of blacks who were recruited by employer groups for work in wartime factories and defense plants. As they crowded the cities, however, African-Americans encountered the resentment of Northern whites. Emotions festered; fear grew.

News of a race riot on July 2, 1917, in East St. Louis, Illinois, made headlines in newspapers all over the country. More than forty blacks had been killed and thousands driven from their homes by angry mobs who set neighborhoods on fire as National Guardsmen looked on. Ida had to see for herself what had happened.

Three days later, she stepped off the train in East St. Louis onto a platform that was empty except for one guardsman. Although warned that it was not safe for a black to be seen in the city, she refused to leave. What she felt as the train left without her has not been recorded, but fear must have been mixed equally with her resolve.

Ida Wells-Barnett walked to city hall alone, hoping to find someone in authority with whom she could tour the burned-out areas of the city. No one seemed to be willing or interested in talking to her, however, and she was ignored in a city still bristling with hostility.

Finally, Ida saw a group of black women boarding a Red Cross truck, accompanied by an armed guard, and joined them. They were returning to their ruined homes to gather what was left of their belongings. As she rode through the devastated areas, she saw firsthand the damage done by the riot, felt the women's fear and anguish, and angrily reported her findings to the governor in Springfield.

Wells-Barnett later returned to East St. Louis twice. By this time the investigation centered on a group of black men who had tried to defend themselves, rather than on the instigators of the riot. Eventually, eleven blacks were convicted of murder and given long prison terms while the white people involved received short ones.

Incensed at one more violent act of discrimination, she began to write a series of articles for the *Chicago Defender* to set the record straight about this latest outrage against her people. Public opinion eventually came around to favor the African-Americans wrongly accused, but the wheels of justice ground more slowly. Ten long years passed before the black men were pardoned by the governor of Illinois.

Ida Wells-Barnett was still reeling from the news of the riots in East St. Louis when more disturbing news reached her. In August 1917, black soldiers waiting near Houston, Texas, to be shipped overseas had reportedly shot and killed a number of whites. According to firsthand reports, the soldiers had been provoked by the whites until the soldiers lost control and shot their tormentors.

The soldiers were quickly court-martialed without appeal; nineteen of them were hanged and many more sentenced to life imprisonment. She was shocked to see how quickly the government moved in this case and began to plan a memorial service for the dead soldiers. To publicize it, she ordered buttons to be made, imprinted with the words, *In Memorial Martyred Negro Soldiers*. The buttons were given to anyone who asked for them.

Not long after, Wells-Barnett received a visit from two Secret Service agents who told her that if she continued to hand out the buttons, she faced arrest and jail. Ida asked what the charge would be. "Treason," she was told. "Why?" she asked. "Because you have criticized the government," came the answer. "Yes," she replied, "and the government deserves to be criticized."[2]

Although the Secret Service agents demanded that she turn over the rest of the buttons to them, she refused, and they left. Nothing more was said as Ida continued to distribute the buttons and wore one herself, for years. Twenty years later, the Houston soldiers who had been imprisoned were pardoned by President Franklin D. Roosevelt.

Wells-Barnett became increasingly active in the Equal Rights League, attending a national meeting held in New York in September. The following year, 1918, the league met in Chicago, at her invitation. It was now apparent that the war in Europe soon would end, and plans were made to have adequate African-American representation at the peace conference which would follow.

On the morning of November 11, 1918, Germany accepted peace terms proposed by the Allies, and World War I ended. A conference to be held in Paris, beginning in January, was scheduled to draw up the peace settlement. Wells-Barnett was one of eleven delegates selected to represent the black point of view at the conference. All eleven delegates, including William Monroe Trotter, were denied passports. According to Wells-Barnett, even he would not have gone had he not disguised himself as a cook and found employment on a ship going to France.

She returned to Chicago and moved to a magnificent home the family had bought on Grand Boulevard. The house contained eight rooms, complete with parquet floors, marble sinks, and a third-floor ballroom which became an apartment for their son Herman and his wife, Fione. The Barnetts were at a point in their lives where they were more secure financially and could enjoy the comforts they had earned. It was interrupted, however, by the attitude of white property owners in the neighborhood who resented the black intrusion, not only of the Barnetts but of other African-American families as well.

A series of bombings of black homes signaled what was to come. In an effort to ward off certain disaster, Wells-Barnett wrote to the *Chicago Tribune*, pleading with city officials to do something. She said, "...set the wheels of justice in motion before it is too late and Chicago be disgraced by the bloody outrages that have disgraced East St. Louis."[3]

For a while nothing happened, and it looked as if disaster had been averted. Then on Sunday, July 29, 1919,[4] a black youngster who had been swimming at a Lake Michigan beach was attacked by a group of white boys and drowned during the fight. The incident was reported to the police, but no one was punished for it.

Wells-Barnett attended a meeting of Chicago ministers who demanded action on this case. They also urged protection of all blacks in the city until tempers had cooled. Clashes couldn't be averted, however, and soon the small fights throughout the city erupted into one large riot that became a race war. For over five days armed mobs ruled the city, and no one was safe. In the Second and Third Wards of the city, called the black belt, African-American men formed human barricades to repel hoodlums as they attempted to set fire to homes and businesses. Although the Barnett family stayed indoors during the rioting, Ida herself patrolled the streets day and night, gathering evidence for the investigation that would follow.

When the fighting stopped, twenty-three blacks and fifteen whites were dead, and more than five hundred people were badly injured. The Chicago race riot had ended. Citizens cautiously began to stir around the city once more, cleaning up the debris and attempting to conciliate a peace. A committee, organized almost immediately, studied the reasons for the riot. It concluded that lack of housing for blacks presented the major problem. Out of necessity, the increasing African-American population had spread from the black belt and caused resentment in white neighbors. The explosive situation became a smoldering powder keg. The boy's death at the hands of a white gang ignited the riot, and the nation's "red summer" of twenty-five major riots continued.

However, before the country could draw a collective sigh, another race riot began in Elaine, Arkansas.

Sharecroppers in the rural areas were being asked to accept a low, unfair price for their cotton, so they had met to organize a union. Once the meeting became known, whites from the surrounding area, and as far away as Mississippi and Tennessee, converged to begin killing the blacks indiscriminately. Rather than arrest the armed whites, the lawmen arrested hundreds of black men and women who were herded into a compound and not allowed representation or communication with anyone else. Called "black revolutionists," they were soon charged with attempting to murder white citizens and steal their land. In a trial that lasted less than an hour, twelve blacks were condemned to death, and sixty-seven were sentenced to long prison terms.

Ida Wells-Barnett had been an active member of the Equal Rights League, which William Monroe Trotter had founded, since she joined in 1913. When the troubles in Arkansas began, she attempted to work through the Chicago chapter. But she grew impatient with what seemed to her to be their slow response. Thus when Oscar DePriest and the People's Movement asked her to discuss what should be done about this latest race riot, she addressed their group at once.

With them, she organized protest meetings and wrote articles for the *Chicago Defender*, calling on the government to intercede and appealing to all readers to aid the victims by contributing to a defense fund. Soon her columns and letters, which she wrote to congressmen as well as to the governor of Arkansas, began to have an effect. The governor called for a conference of black and white people, then pledged that he would see to it that the African-Americans sentenced to death received a new trial.

When Ida Wells-Barnett returned to the Equal Rights League for a meeting to report on what had happened, the other members denounced her for taking matters into her own hands. She explained that, with men under the threat of hanging, she felt there was little time to be lost. The group listened but nevertheless passed a law suspending any member who acted independently. She walked out of the meeting and never worked with the League again.

The Arkansas case dragged on without resolution. Three times, gallows were built to hang the twelve condemned men, and three times their lives were saved by last-minute appeals.

Meanwhile, Wells-Barnett continued to encounter more problems, some closer to home. Although she had given up her position as probation officer in 1916, she continued to work with young black men and women who needed help through the Negro Fellowship League and the social center she began in 1910. It was not easy without financial aid now that the income from her job had ceased.

Since the end of World War I, Ida Wells-Barnett had employed veterans in the reading room of the center, hoping to give many of them a fresh start in a new life. This was not entirely successful. Earlier she had placed a man and his wife in charge of the employment office. In the four months they were there, they did not pay the rent nor were they very successful in finding jobs for clients.

Then, the week before Thanksgiving, the man and his wife moved out, taking with them most of the furnishings which belonged to the center. Wells-Barnett was left with debts to pay and a decision to make. She paid off the debts and reluctantly closed the center, which had been in existence for ten years. Had it served a purpose? She tried to believe it had.

One week later, on December 15, 1920, Wells-Barnett went to the hospital for a serious operation. Many weeks passed before she recovered, and when, characteristically, she tried to resume an active life much too soon, she experienced a serious setback. It would be more than a year before her health returned. Meanwhile, at the age of fifty-eight, she finally had time to contemplate what she had done with her life thus far and what she should try to accomplish with the rest of it.

11
ALWAYS VIGILANT

Ida Wells-Barnett's health continued to improve slowly. She spent eight weeks in bed after her setback and many more just resting at home after that. During this time she continued to review her goals, her priorities, and her accomplishments. She also may have suffered from a certain amount of depression as well. Otherwise she would not have come to the conclusion that she had "nothing to show for all those years of toil and labor."[1] Realistically, she had to know she had accomplished much in improving the lives of African-Americans, even though the United States still continued on an unsettled course in the area of civil rights.

Wells-Barnett stated in her autobiography, "Eternal vigilance is the price of liberty,"[2] and, as her strength returned, so did her vigilance. Finally, in January 1922, she no longer could sit idly by. Once more, Ida Wells-Barnett went into action. The Arkansas race riots were still unresolved and with characteristic determination she decided to find out why.

Ida Wells-Barnett traveled by train to Little Rock,

Arkansas, arriving early on a Sunday morning and went directly to the home of the wife of one of the men who had been sentenced to death. (She had received a letter from him, with his home address on it.) Ida found other wives and relatives there, preparing to go to the jail to visit their sons and husbands. She decided to go with them, claiming to be a cousin, and had no trouble being admitted to the prison.

Inside the jail, she was introduced to officials as the cousin of Mrs. Moore, a prisoner's wife. As she walked from one cell to another, putting her hand through the bars so the prisoners could shake it, Mrs. Moore would whisper, "This is Mrs. Barnett, from Chicago."[3] The prisoners knew her by reputation and looked as if they would shout out their amazement and joy at seeing this famous lady. But they also knew the value of silence and of keeping her presence a secret from the guards. The prison guards never caught on that the short, somewhat plump lady with graying hair was the fiery activist for human rights, Ida B. Wells-Barnett.

Wells-Barnett was able to ask questions of each prisoner and receive their whispered answers. She asked them about their lives prior to imprisonment, where they had farmed, what crops they'd grown, and what had happened to their property since they had been jailed.

They also spoke of life in prison. The jail in Little Rock was considerably better than the jails in Helena and Elaine, Arkansas, where the black rioters had been under constant threat of being lynched. They also had been beaten and given electric shocks to force them into confessions about their so-called crimes.

Finally, before she left, the men sang songs for their visitors that they had composed themselves. Even the warden of the prison came and listened to them. After the last notes faded away, Ida went up to the men and spoke quietly, telling them to pray about life and freedom instead of death and dying.

Then she returned to the home where she was a guest and wrote about her conversations with the imprisoned men. She had been unable to take notes while visiting them and depended on her memory for all the details. After visiting the prisoners' attorney and the committee in charge of raising funds in their behalf, she returned to Chicago and wrote a pamphlet called *The Arkansas Race Riot*. One thousand copies were printed and distributed, primarily in Arkansas. Not until the following year, 1923, did the Supreme Court finally rule that the men were imprisoned unlawfully and released them over a period of many months.

Restored to good health, Wells-Barnett displayed a vigor and strength not found in many women in their early sixties in that day. She was never without a project. Once she saw the Arkansas prisoners released to begin new lives, she turned to other activities. After thirty years, she was again elected president of the Ida B. Wells Woman's Club. In addition she soon began to lecture on behalf of the National Association of Colored Women, hoping to find new talent and support for this organization. Her campaign found modest support but much opposition. This was due primarily to her lack of diplomacy when she denounced the "do nothings" in the group.

In 1924, when the national organization of the association convened in Chicago, Ida Wells-Barnett decided to campaign for the presidency against Mary McLeod Bethune, who had been vice president. Ida, however, could not muster enough support and lost the election. Although she was disappointed, she continued to work with area and statewide clubs, in both black and white women's groups.

In 1925 Ida Wells-Barnett and her husband, Ferdinand, moved from the large home on Grand Boulevard into a five-room apartment on Garfield Boulevard. Like those of many older couples, their incomes had

108

decreased, and all of their children but one were married and had gone on to homes of their own. The Barnetts simply no longer needed or could afford a large house.

The smaller apartment seemed to suit their needs just fine. Now Ida slowed down long enough to welcome her grandchildren for a visit and to spend some time with her sisters. Other women who came to call were intent on business as she once had been, seeking her assistance and advice rather than her friendship. Social occasions were rare.

Ida Wells-Barnett remained keenly interested in politics. Although there were now six black representatives to the state legislature and the first black congressman to be elected since Reconstruction came from Illinois, Ida was not pleased with their performances. She found they paid little attention to the needs of the people in their districts, with problems of unemployment, hunger, and homelessness being largely ignored. In 1929, at the age of sixty-seven, she decided to run for the state senate.

Ida Wells-Barnett was affiliated with the Republican party but ran as an independent when the Republicans refused to endorse her candidacy. She found support from women in the many organizations she had served, and she spoke at churches and at other club meetings, looking for more votes. However, she finished a poor third in the race. Disappointed once again, she nevertheless proved that a black woman of that day and generation could make herself heard. Once again, she provided inspiration and motivation to her gender and race to do even more than was expected.

During the years following her surgery, she began writing her memoirs, finally realizing that her life and thoughts needed to be put down for others to know about and to emulate. Carefully and thoughtfully, she wrote and rewrote and corrected. But the autobiography was left unfinished, in midsentence. The last words were: "I also received some beautiful letters from members of the board of directors thanking us for calling attention to what was go–"[4]

On March 21, 1931, Ida went to town to do some shopping but came home not feeling well. Two days later, she was rushed to the hospital, seriously ill with uremic poisoning, an accumulation in the blood of substances normally excreted in the urine. The infection spread so quickly that the doctors in attendance could do nothing. Ida Wells-Barnett died on Wednesday, March 25, on the thirty-fifth birthday of her oldest son, Charles.

The *Chicago Defender* paid tribute to her memory, describing her as "elegant, striking, always well groomed …regal."[5] Those words, while true, miss the mark completely on what Ida B. Wells-Barnett's life was all about and what should be remembered about her. She was devoted to the cause of justice, dedicated to the ideals of equal rights, and demanded the very best of everyone whose lives she touched.

Ida Wells-Barnett was a strong, forceful, compelling person, impatient with those who did not display her invincibility. Her wit was sharp, and at times her tongue was even sharper. If she could have been more moderate in tone and less derisive in manner, her popularity during her lifetime may have been greater and her place in history more renowned. But that wouldn't have been the person she was. The work was more important than the woman.

Her family spoke of her with awe and reverence. Never once, according to a relative, did one member of the family say a bad thing about her, although her children chose not to emulate her public life. Her daughter, Alfreda, said, "we all make choices,"[6] and she decided not to become a public person as her mother had been. Instead she chose to raise a family while having a career that did not make headlines.

Ida Wells-Barnett had made headlines. Always a

mover and a shaker, she acted with initiative and conviction and, much of the time, alone. When she launched a campaign against lynching, it fomented a campaign for civil and equal rights for blacks and women that is not over, even today. And she did it in a most compelling way. By framing the problem in economic terms, she explained that, as long as blacks and women were kept in their places, white men held the power and were reluctant to give it up.

Wells-Barnett pointed out that during the Civil War, white women were left alone on plantations with only slaves for protection. There was never a cry of rape then. Only when black men became economic rivals to white men after the war was the cry of assault raised. She appealed to the consciousness of the English-speaking world; in fact, she became the public conscience when the world seemed not to have any. She reminded everyone that this was their fight and they were in collusion if they did not act. Ida Wells-Barnett's campaign against lynching is considered by many to be the actual beginning of the Civil Rights Movement.

She is not forgotten. In 1941, the Chicago Housing Authority changed the name of a housing project to the Ida B. Wells Homes. Her diary lies in its cornerstone. The development covers about forty-seven acres and houses more than 7,000 persons. In 1950 the city of Chicago named her as one of the city's most outstanding women in its history. In 1974, a plaque was placed by the Department of the Interior on the Grand Boulevard house where Ida Wells-Barnett once lived, designating it as a National Historic Landmark. Finally, a postage stamp was issued in 1990 in her honor, and a public television program documented her life in an hour-long presentation.

Ida worked tirelessly and wrote endlessly on the problems that confronted her, her race, and her gender. Out of all the words, perhaps one sentence she spoke to the prisoners in Little Rock best serves to convey her feelings and philosophy of life as she lived it. After the prisoners had sung for her, Ida Wells-Barnett told them, "Let your songs be songs of faith and hope."[7]

It is a message for everyone.

SOURCE NOTES

CHAPTER 1

1. Stephen B. Oates, *With Malice Toward None* (New York: Harper & Row, 1977), p. 256.
2. Ibid., p. 297.
3. Ibid., p. 307.
4. John Hope Franklin, *Reconstruction After the Civil War* (Chicago: University of Chicago Press, 1961), p. 2.
5. The eleven confederate states were, in order of secession: South Carolina, Georgia, Florida, Alabama, Mississippi, Louisiana, Texas, Virginia, North Carolina, Tennessee, and Arkansas.
6. Franklin, p. 39.
7. Ida B. Wells-Barnett, *Crusade For Justice*, edited by Alfreda M. Duster (hereafter cited as *Crusade For Justice*) (Chicago: University of Chicago Press, 1970), p. 9.

CHAPTER 2

1. Dorothy Sterling, *Black Foremothers: Three Lives* (hereafter cited as *Black Foremothers*) (New York: McGraw Hill Book Company, 1979), p. 66.
2. *Crusade For Justice*, p. 14.
3. *Black Foremothers*, p. 68.
4. Ibid., p. 71.
5. *Crusade For Justice*, p. 19.

6. Quoted in Mildred I. Thompson, *Ida B. Wells-Barnett: An Exploratory Study of An American Black Woman, 1893-1930* (hereafter cited as *Ida B. Wells-Barnett*) (Brooklyn, New York: Carlson Publishing Company, 1990), p. 14, in Tennessee, "Reports of Cases Argued and Determined in the Supreme Court of Tennessee" by George Wesley Pickle (Nashville: Marshall and Bruce Stationers and Printers, 1887), pp. 614, 615.

CHAPTER 3

1. *Crusade For Justice*, p. 24.
2. Ibid., p. 23.
3. I. Garland Penn, *The Afro-American Press and Its Editors* (hereafter cited as *The Afro-American Press*) (Springfield, Massachusetts: Wiley and Company, Publishers, 1891), p. 408.
4. Ibid., p. 23.
5. *Black Foremothers*, p. 74.
6. Ibid., p. 74.
7. Ibid., p. 75.
8. *Crusade For Justice*, p. 33.
9. *The Afro-American Press*, p. 187.
10. *Black Foremothers*, p. 74.
11. *Crusade For Justice*, p. 49.
12. Quoted in Mary M. B. Hutton, "The Rhetoric of Ida B. Wells: The Genesis of the Anti-Lynch Movement (Indiana University, Doctoral Dissertation, 1975), (hereafter cited as "The Rhetoric of Ida B. Wells") p. 30, *Our Day* (January-June 1893), pp. 334, 335.
13. *Crusade For Justice*, p. 52.
14. Quoted in Thompson, *Ida B. Wells-Barnett, Free Speech*, May 21, 1893, p. 29.
15. *Crusade For Justice*, p. 61.

CHAPTER 4

1. Quoted in Hutton, "The Rhetoric of Ida B. Wells," p. 16, James Elbert Cutler, "Lynch Law: An Investigation Into the History of Lynching in the United States" (New York: Negro Universities Press, 1969), p. 59.

114

2. Ibid., p. 17.
3. Sadie Iola Daniel, *Women Builders* (hereafter cited as *Women Builders*) (Associated Publishers: Washington, D. C., 1970), pp. 263, 264.
4. Quoted in Hutton, "The Rhetoric of Ida B. Wells," p. 21, Frederick Douglass, "Speech at Washington," *Anti-Caste*, VII (April-May 1895), p. 11.
5. Quoted in Sterling, *Black Foremothers*, p. 83, *New York Age*, June 25, 1892.
6. Quoted in *The Crisis*, p. 540, Paula Giddings, "Highlights of the History of Black Women 1910-1980," (hereafter cited as "Highlights of the History of Black Women").
7. *Crusade For Justice*, p. 80.
8. Paula Giddings, "Highlights of the History of Black Women," p. 540.
9. *Black Foremothers*, p. 85.
10. *Crusade For Justice*, p. 85.
11. Ibid., p. 88.
12. Quoted in Hutton, "The Rhetoric of Ida B. Wells," p. 63, Ferdinand L. Barnett, "The Reason Why the Colored American Is Not in the World's Columbian Exposition" (Chicago, *Ida B. Wells*, 1893), pp. 73, 79.
13. *Crusade For Justice*, p. 117.

CHAPTER 5

1. *Black Foremothers*, p. 96.
2. *Crusade For Justice*, p. 64.
3. Quoted in Hutton, "The Rhetoric of Ida B. Wells," p. 65, "A Sermon on Ibsen—A Coloured Woman in the Pulpit," *Christian World*, 38 (March 15, 1894), p. 187.
4. *Women Builders*, p. 274.
5. *Crusade For Justice*, p. 179.
6. Ibid., p. 179.
7. Quoted in Thompson, *Ida B. Wells-Barnett*, p. 56, *New York Voice*, October 23, 1890.
8. Quoted in Hutton, "The Rhetoric of Ida B. Wells," p. 103, *New York Voice*, October 23, 1890.
9. *Crusade For Justice*, p. 151.
10. *Women Builders*, p. 278.
11. Ibid., p. 276.

12. *Black Foremothers*, p. 91.
13. Ibid., p. 92.
14. *Women Builders*, p. 276.
15. *Black Foremothers*, p. 92.

CHAPTER 6

1. *Crusade For Justice*, p. 212.
2. Ibid., p. 218.
3. *Black Foremothers*, p. 95.
4. *Crusade For Justice*, p. 226.
5. Wells-Barnett, *A Red Record: Tabulated Statistics and Alleged Causes of Lynchings in the United States*, printed in *On Lynchings* (New York: Arno Press, 1969), also *Crusade For Justice*, p. xxii.
6. Quoted in Paula Giddings, *Essence*, p. 142, "A Red Record."
7. *Black Foremothers*, pp. 93, 94.
8. *Crusade For Justice*, p. 232.
9. Ibid., p. 238.
10. Ralph Nelson Davis, "The Negro Newspaper in Chicago" (Chicago: Chicago University Master of Arts Dissertation, 1939), p. 11.
11. Ibid., p. 18.
12. Ibid.

CHAPTER 7

1. *Crusade For Justice*, p. 242.
2. Ibid., p. 242.
3. *Black Foremothers*, p. 96.
4. Ibid., p. 97.
5. Ibid.
6. *Crusade For Justice*, p. 248.
7. Ibid., p. 248.
8. Ibid., p. 243.
9. Ibid.
10. Ibid., p. 248.
11. *Black Foremothers*, p. 99.

12. Ibid., p. 100.
13. *World Book Encyclopedia* Volume 18 (Chicago: Scott Fetzger Company, 1988 Edition), p. 754.
14. *Crusade For Justice*, p. 255.

CHAPTER 8

1. Barbara Belford, *Brilliant Bylines* (New York: Columbia University Press, 1986), p. 91.
2. *Black Foremothers*, p. 101.
3. Ibid., p. 102.
4. Charles Flint Kellogg, *NAACP: A History of the National Association for the Advancement of Colored People*: Volume I (1909-1920) (hereafter cited as *NAACP*) (Baltimore: Johns Hopkins Press, 1967), p. 9.
5. Ibid., p. 9.
6. Ibid., p. 19.
7. *Black Foremothers*, p. 104.

CHAPTER 9

1. *Black Foremothers*, p. 105.
2. *Crusade For Justice*, p. 311.
3. Ibid., p. 311.
4. Ibid.
5. *Black Foremothers*, p. 106.
6. Ibid., p. 107.
7. *Crusade For Justice*, p. 326.
8. *NAACP*, p. 92.
9. *Black Foremothers*, p. 110.
10. Ibid.
11. Stephen R. Fox, *The Guardian of Boston: William Monroe Trotter* (New York: Atheneum, 1970), p. 180.
12. Ibid.

CHAPTER 10

1. Arthur Walworth, *Woodrow Wilson: World Prophet*, Volume 2 (New York London Toronto: Longmans, Green & Company, 1958), p. 99.

2. *Crusade For Justice*, p. 370.

3. *Black Foremothers*, p. 112.

4. This date is sometimes given as July 27, 1919.

CHAPTER 11

1. *Crusade For Justice*, p. 414.

2. Ibid., p. 401.

3. Ibid.

4. Ibid., p. 419.

5. Langston Hughes, *Famous Negroes of America* (New York: Dodd Mead and Company, 1958), p. 162.

6. Dr. Troy Duster, telephone interview, November, 1990.

7. *Crusade For Justice*, p. 403.

GLOSSARY

Abolitionist—A person who believes in legally abolishing, or ending, slavery.

Accommodationist—A person who is willing to adapt, tolerate, or agree to a situation in order to get along with others.

Activist—A person who practices vigorous action to achieve political or social goals.

Alderman—A member of a municipal body.

Amnesty—A general pardon for offenses against a government.

Anarchy—A society without government or law.

Bestir—To arouse to action.

Draft—A selection of individuals for military service.

Emancipation Proclamation—Edict by Abraham Lincoln which freed all slaves in areas in rebellion against the United States. Slavery was completely abolished in the United States with the adoption of the thirteenth Amendment to the Constitution in 1865.

Equivalency—Philosophy practiced by those who believe in equality for everyone.

Franchise—The right to vote.

Grandfather clause—Method of disenfranchising blacks by giving the vote only to males who had served in the military or to those who had voted before 1876.

Habeas corpus—A legal writ requiring a person to be brought before a judge or court. It was used as a protection against illegal imprisonment.

Jim Crow—Term used in the United States to describe laws and practices which maintained segregation and discrimination against blacks.

Lyceum—A program which provides education through lectures, concerts.

Lynching—To kill a person by mob action without legal authority.

Masons—Fraternal order or society with secret laws governing the association.

Melee—A confusing, general, hand-to-hand fight.

Mentor—A wise and trusted teacher or counselor.

Militant—A person who vigorously and aggressively supports a cause or action.

Party platform—Standards or beliefs of a political party during an election to gain governmental control.

Probation officer—A person appointed by the court to supervise offenders who have been conditionally released from prison.

Ratify—To approve or confirm a formal sanction.

Sapphira—A female liar. In Biblical times, Sapphira Ananias, and her husband were struck dead for lying about the price of a piece of land they sold in order to give the proceeds to the church.

Segregation—Separation from the rest of society because of religious or racial differences.

Settlement house—A welfare establishment in an underprivileged section of a city.

Sexism—Discrimination because of sex.

Stamp masters—After the Stamp Act was passed in the colonies in 1764, stamp masters, or distributors, handled the sale of the stamped paper.

Suffrage—The right to vote.

Temperance—Moderation or total abstinence from drinking alcoholic beverages.

Understanding clause—Another method of preventing blacks from exercising the right to vote. Certain sections of the Constitution were read to them, and they were expected to explain the passages, as interpreted by whites administering the "test."

W.C.T.U.—Woman's Christian Temperance Union. An organization founded in 1874 to work for public education against the use of alcohol. Frances Willard was its second president.

White supremacists—Caucasians who advocate supremacy of their race over others, particularly blacks.

Yellow fever—Also known as yellow jack, it is an acute viral disease occurring primarily in warm climates and transmitted by a mosquito.

BIBLIOGRAPHY

BOOKS

Belford, Barbara. *Brilliant Bylines*, New York: Columbia
　University Press, 1986.

Broderick, Francis I. *W.E.B. DuBois: Negro Leader in a Time of
　Crisis*, Stanford: Stanford University Press, 1959.

Carter, Hodding. *A Vanishing America: The Life and Times of the
　Small Town*, edited by Thomas C. Wheeler. New York:
　Holt, Rinehart and Winston, 1964.

Daniel, Sadie Iola. *Women Builders*, Washington, D. C.:
　Associated Publishers, 1970.

Foner, Philip S. *Frederick Douglass: A Biography*, New York:
　Citadel Press, 1964.

Fox, Stephen R. *The Guardian of Boston: William Monroe
　Trotter*, New York: Atheneum, 1970.

Franklin, John Hope. *Reconstruction After the Civil War*, Chicago
　History of Civilization, edited by Daniel Boorstin.
　Chicago: University of Chicago Press, 1961.

Hughes, Langston. *Famous Negro Heroes of America*, New York:
　Dodd Mead and Company, 1958.

Kellogg, Charles Flint. *NAACP: A History of the National
　Association of Colored People*: Volume 1 (1909-1920),
　Baltimore: Johns Hopkins Press, 1967.

Lerner, Gerda. *Black Women in White America*, New York:
　Vintage, 1973.

Oates, Stephen B. *With Malice Toward None*, New York: Harper
　& Row, 1977.

Owsley, Frank Lawrence. *King Cotton Diplomacy: Foreign Relations of the Conference States of America.* 2nd ed. revised by Harriet Chappell Owsley, Chicago: University of Chicago Press, 1959.

Penn, I. Garland. *The Afro-American Press and Its Editors,* Springfield, Massachusetts: Wiley and Company, 1891.

Smear, Howard. *Blood Justice,* New York and Oxford: Oxford University Press, 1986.

Sterling, Dorothy. *Black Foremothers: Three Lives,* Old Westbury, New York, San Francisco, St. Louis: The Feminist Press and McGraw Hill Book Company, 1979.

Thompson, Mildred I. *Ida B. Wells-Barnett: An Exploratory Study of an American Black Woman, 1893-1930,* Brooklyn, New York: Carlson Publishing, Inc., 1990.

Truman, Margaret. *Women of Courage,* New York: William Morrow, 1976.

Walworth, Arthur. *Woodrow Wilson: World Prophet,* Volume 2, New York London Toronto: Longmans, Green & Company, 1958.

Wells-Barnett, Ida. B. *Crusade For Justice,* edited by Alfreda M. Duster. Chicago and London: University of Chicago Press, 1970.

DISSERTATIONS

Hutton, Mary Magdelene Boone. "The Rhetoric of Ida B. Wells: The Genesis of the Anti-Lynch Movement," Bloomington, Indiana, Indiana University: Department of Speech, Graduate School, 1975.

Nelson, Ralph. "The Negro Newspaper in Chicago," Chicago: University of Chicago, 1939.

MAGAZINES

The Crisis, December, 1960, pp. 540, 545, "Highlights of the History of Black Women," 1910-1980, Paula Giddings.

The Christian Century, March 15, 1989, pp. 285, 286, *Ida B. Wells-Barnett: An Afro-American Prophet,* Emilie M. Townes.

Essence, February, 1988, pp. 76, 142, 146, *Woman Warrior,* Paula Giddings.

REFERENCE

Encyclopedia of American Biography, 1974.
World Book Encyclopedia Volumes 2 and 18, Scott Fetzger
Company, Chicago, 1988 edition.

INDEX

125

127